Oct 26, 1983

To Frank

with the hope that it is not
true that " we learn from
history that we learn nothing from history"

with love

Rosalie and Bob

The Middle East Conflicts

From 1945 to the Present

The Middle East Conflicts

From 1945 to the Present

Consultant editor John Pimlott

CRESCENT BOOKS · New York

Consultant editor
John Pimlott is the author of a recently published book on the *B–29 Superfortress* and co-author of *Strategy and Tactics of War*. He has written a book on the *Battle of the Bulge* and has contributed to an encyclopedia of *World War II*. He is Senior Lecturer in the Department of War Studies and International Affairs at Sandhurst.

The authors
Ian Beckett is a senior lecturer in the Department of War Studies and International Affairs at Sandhurst. He is the co-author of *Politicians and Defence*.

Simon Innes was educated at Warwick University and Sandhurst, and has done particular research into the problems of the late 1940s.

Eric Morris is Deputy Head of the Department of War Studies and International Affairs at the Royal Military Academy Sandhurst. His books include *Berlin and the Cold War, The Russian Navy, Myth and Reality* and a *History of Tanks*.

Michael Orr has been a lecturer at Sandhurst since 1969. He is the author of *Dettingen 1743* and has contributed many articles to military publications. He is a specialist on the Soviet Army.

David Rosser-Owen is at the Royal United Services Institute, London. He has contributed to many specialist publications, and his main area of interest is in the modern Arab World.

Acknowledgements
Photographs were supplied by Associated Press, Black Star, Deutsche Presse Agentur, Eshel-Dramit Ltd, John Frost Newspaper Collection, Gamma, Haganah Archive, Robert Hunt Library, Imperial War Museum, Israeli Government Press Office, Israeli Government Tourist Office, Keystone Press Agency, Novosti Press Agency, Pilot Press, Popperfoto, Rex Features, *Soldier* magazine, Frank Spooner, John Topham, United Press International, Brigadier Peter Young, Zionist Archives. Maps and diagrams were drawn by Gordon Beckett, Graham Bingham, Paul Bryant, Tony Gibbons, Keith Harmer, Mike Holland, Ed Stuart.

Editors Ashley Brown, Richard Williams
Designer Mick Hodson

Printed in Italy
ISBN 0-517-408740
Library of Congress Catalog Card Number: 83-70452
h g f e d c b a

Contents

Introduction

The 'Middle East' is a very imprecise term, belonging to a time when Europe was regarded as the centre of the world and other areas were described according to their direction and distance from London, Paris or Berlin. It was first used in the early twentieth century to denote the 'buffer zone' of Persia (Iran), Iraq, the Persian (Arabian) Gulf and Afghanistan which lay between the expanding empires of Britain and Russia, as distinct from the Near East of the Ottoman (Turkish) Empire and the Far East of India, Southeast Asia, and China.

With the collapse of the Ottoman Empire and the sudden insularity of post-revolutionary Russia at the end of the First World War, the need for such distinctions declined, but the term 'Middle East' remained in general usage. It was gradually expanded in scope to include the ex-Turkish possessions of the so-called Fertile Crescent (modern-day Israel, Jordan, Syria and Lebanon), as well as the British protectorate of Egypt. As such, it was never the same as the 'Arab world' (for which the North African states of Morocco, Algeria, Tunisia and Libya, together with Sudan, would have to be added and the non-Arab states of Israel, Iran and Afghanistan excluded) or the 'Islamic world' (which would have to include Turkey, Pakistan and a number of states in Africa and even Southeast Asia), so in the end any precise definition has to reflect the needs of the definer. For the purposes of this book, the 'Middle East' denotes the specific countries of Egypt, Israel, Jordan, Syria, Iraq, Lebanon, Iran, Saudi Arabia and the Gulf States; a region which may be described in general terms as the land-mass linking the continents of Africa, Europe and Asia.

The area, as defined, had suffered a long history of rivalry and conflict, of which the period since 1945 is merely the latest chapter. On analysis it is not difficult to see why this should be so. The Middle East occupies a position of immense geo-strategic significance which invites a high degree of interference by outside powers intent upon personal control or the denial of influence to potential or actual rivals. In terms of world trade, the routes which pass through the region by both land and sea constitute the centre of a vast network, the disruption or loss of which would destroy integral parts of the international commercial framework. Throughout history the Middle East has offered links between the three surrounding continents and in more modern times, with the opening of the Suez Canal and the discovery and exploitation of oil, has gained its own intrinsic importance. To European powers especially, with their heavy dependence upon trade and raw materials, the area has for a long time been a natural focus of attention.

The Ottoman decline

So long as the Turks maintained effective rule in the region, such European interest had little direct impact, but as soon as the Ottoman Empire began to show signs of weakness both the British and French, reflecting their global, colonial interests, stepped in. The process began with the building of the Suez Canal in the 1860s and thereafter both powers did all they could to ensure control not just of the land approaches to the Canal but also of the sea-lanes leading into and out of the Red Sea. Such control was essential to ensure the protection of the Canal as a link between Europe and the Far East, and in the ensuing burst of colonial activity in the Middle East, Britain emerged as the dominant power.

By the beginning of the First World War in 1914, Great Britain had secured possession of Cyprus and the northern approaches to the Suez Canal in the eastern Mediterranean, was firmly in control of Egypt and Sudan, protecting the landward approaches to the waterway from the west, and held territory (at Aden and in Somaliland) on both banks of the strategically important Babel Mandeb Straits, where the Red Sea joins the Indian Ocean. By comparison the French, although in possession of Djibouti (the Territory of the Afars and Issas) to the north of Somaliland, had failed to occupy any areas of great strategic value. Nevertheless, with continued involvement in the operation of the Suez Canal itself through the Anglo-French Suez Canal Company, and a record of interest in the Turkish territory of Syria through support for the pro-European Christian community around Mount Lebanon, it was apparent that the French were maintaining an influence.

The European powers were therefore in an ideal position to exploit the collapse of the Ottoman Empire, which occurred as Turkey suffered defeat during the First World War, and at the end of that conflict, as victorious allies, they were able to take over large areas of the Middle East in accordance with the terms of the secret Sykes-Picot Agreement of 1916. Once again, however, the British dominated the key strategic locations, having conducted military campaigns against the Turks during the war which left them in possession of important parts of the Fertile Crescent. A degree of national self-determination was afforded to Arab tribesmen who had contributed to the British victory – a policy that was to lead to the emergence of Saudi Arabia by 1932 – but the important approaches to the Suez Canal from the east (Palestine, Transjordan and Iraq) were transferred to British administration as League of Nations 'mandates', leaving the less strategically significant region of 'Greater Syria' to the French.

The mandates were designed to act as preludes to eventual independence and in the cases of Iraq and to a lesser extent Transjordan this had been implemented by 1930, but to the British Palestine was too important to relinquish. At the same time the French made no moves to grant independence to Greater Syria, even going so far as to create a new, Christian-dominated, coastal state of Lebanon in 1920. The European presence in the Middle East seemed to be permanent.

The situation changed as a result of the Second World War. Initially it was French influence that waned, particularly after the pro-German Vichy regime had been physically ousted from Lebanon and Syria in 1941 by British and Free French forces. The Free French, reacting to pressures from their allies (particularly the United States after December 1941) and aware that they lacked the strength to follow any alternative policy, granted independence to their mandated territories, withdrawing entirely from the region in 1946.

British withdrawal

This left the British as the only European power in the Middle East, but their days were numbered. In response to the nationalism engendered by the Second World War and the crippling financial cost of maintaining a global presence, they gradually loosened their grip on empire. After the granting of independence to India, Pakistan, Burma and Ceylon in 1947–48, the Suez Canal became less essential as a colonial link and this was reflected in the decision, made under the additional pressure of a Jewish terrorist campaign against continued British rule, to relinquish the mandate over Palestine in May 1948. Eight years later both the British and the French made a last desperate attempt to reassert their influence by mounting an invasion of Egypt after President Gamal Abdel Nasser's nationalisation of the Suez Canal Company, but their failure to achieve their objectives in the face of world condemnation marked the end of the European era of interference in the Middle East.

But the region was still too important to be left to its own devices and the British and French were replaced immediately by the two superpowers, the United States and the Soviet Union. Their interest in the region may not have been the same as that of the European powers over the previous 70 years, but nothing could alter the importance of the Middle East in geo-strategic terms. Domination of the area by one superpower would undermine the security of the other – if, for example, the Americans controlled the Middle East, Western power would be projected to threaten the southern flank of the Soviet Union and would deny her access to world oceans through the eastern Mediterranean and Suez Canal; if the Soviets dominated the region, the southern tier of the NATO alliance would lie exposed and the vital oil routes would be cut .

Once again, the Middle East could not escape the consequences of its position and although a physical occupation of territory is no longer essential in an age of mobile, long-range armed forces, the fact that both superpowers now play a dangerous power-game in the Middle East, using their respective proxy allies to try and gain advantage, ensures that the pressure of outside interference has not eased. It is a major contributing factor to the high incidence of conflict in the region and one that constitutes a major theme within this book.

Religious differences

But no outside power would be able to interfere in this way unless there were weaknesses to exploit among the indigenous states, and it is an unfortunate characteristic of the Middle East that such weaknesses exist in abundance. The most obvious is the fact that the region contains a plethora of different religious beliefs, most of them mutually hostile. The three main monotheistic religions of the world – the Jewish faith, Christianity and Islam – all have their origins and major shrines in the area and this has led to incessant rivalry and conflict. The Crusades of the twelfth and thirteenth centuries show how this has caused outside interference, but it has also given ample grounds for internal trouble, as Israeli campaigns to gain control of Jerusalem in 1948 and 1967 serve to illustrate.

Even within the Islamic states, differences of doctrine produce bitter rivalries, particularly between the Shi'ite and Sunn'ite sects. The Moslem world is split between Sunn'ites and Shi'ites with the former constituting the majority. The split dates back to the seventh century, and a dispute over who should succeed the prophet Mohammad: the Shi'ites preferred his son-in-law, Ali, while the Sunn'ites turned instead to the prophet's father-in-law, Abu Bakr. Shi'ites constitute majorities in Iran, Iraq, North Yemen and Bahrain, and form substantial minorities in Lebanon, Syria, Turkey, Pakistan and Afghanistan, but most Moslem countries tend to be governed by Sunn'ites. This religious divide is a source of constant division and rivalry in the Moslem world, and is often reflected in the growth of extremist political factions, of which the Ba'athists and Moslem fundamentalists are just two of the better known.

Indeed, the religious and political divisions within the Arab states of the Middle East have probably contributed more to the incidence of violence and conflict than any other single factor, for if these states could ever sink their differences and unite, as so many Arab leaders of the post-1945 period have endeavoured to ensure, they would represent a solid bloc of opposition to the interference of external or non-Arab powers. As it is, their internal problems and lack of basic unity have produced a climate of weakness which leaves the region as a whole extremely vulnerable to exploitation. The nature and extent of these indigenous divisions is the second of the major themes of this book.

The challenge of Zionism

But religious differences have produced another, much more dramatic, result and that is the challenge posed to the Arab states by the establishment and continued existence of the state of Israel. To anyone familiar with the Bible, the fact that a Jewish state existed in the Middle East 2000 years ago is well-known, but the idea of recreating this by setting up a 'homeland' for Jews who wished to escape the anti-semitic repression so prevalent in other countries, dates back only about 100 years. It was the brainchild of the Hungarian Jew, Theodor Herzl, whose book *The Jewish State* led, in the late nineteenth century, to the creation of a politico-religious movement for a return to the 'Israel' of antiquity.

Known as Zionism, this movement had little impact until the trauma of the First World War led the Allied powers to value the influence of the Jews, particularly in their efforts to ensure American entry into the conflict. As the Jews constituted a powerful body within the United States – then as now – their support for the war was essential. At the same time the British, already planning their future administration of Palestine, were not averse to a pro-European Jewish presence in the area, and for this reason were prepared to make certain promises to the Zionists in exchange for their support. These were contained in the now-famous Balfour Declaration of 2 November 1917, in which the British Foreign Secretary, Arthur Balfour, let it be known that his government viewed 'with favour the establishment in Palestine of a national home for the Jewish people', subject to certain conditions designed to safeguard the 'civil and religious rights of the existing non-Jewish communities' in the region.

Unfortunately all this was rather vague and clearly meant different things to different people. To the British it meant allowing a degree of Jewish immigration into Palestine, although never to an extent that would prejudice the rights of the indigenous population; to the Zionists it represented the first step in the creation of an independent Jewish state.

Between 1920 and 1948, when the British withdrew from the area, genuine efforts were made to prevent the emergence of conflict, but to little avail. As

Jewish immigration and purchase of land increased, the Arabs felt threatened, blaming the British for allowing the situation to develop; as the British endeavoured to control the growth of Jewish influence, they came under attack from Zionist guerrilla and terrorist groups. It was an impossible situation and one which must have been handed over to the United Nations with some relief in 1947–48.

The fact that the new state of Israel survived at all after the declaration of independence on 14 May 1948 was as much to do with Arab disunity and outside interference as Jewish military power, but the continued presence of an alien political and religious entity within the Moslem-dominated Middle East has constituted a permanent thorn in the side of the Arab countries. So long as Israel exists, they face the constant reminder that in 1948 they failed to protect their own, and as the exiled Palestinians and the ever-expanding Israelis fight each other, neighbouring states are inevitably drawn in, backed by their respective superpower allies. The results of these Arab-Israeli clashes naturally form the central and most dramatic theme of this book, but it should be borne in mind throughout that without the existence of the other themes – outside interference and internal Arab disunity – the tragedy that has occurred in the Middle East since 1948 would probably have been prevented or at least ameliorated. The causes of conflict are therefore complex and, as a corollary, peaceful solutions are extremely difficult to find. In the end, one cannot escape from the rather depressing conclusion that, as long as the ingredients for violence continue to exist, it is difficult to foresee any lasting peace in the Middle East.

J. L. PIMLOTT

1. The Birth of the New Israel

Probably the most important single factor determining events in Palestine between 1945 and 1948 was the fact that Jewish nationalist and terrorist organisations knew precisely what they wished to achieve while the British government did not. The principal Jewish organisation established under the terms of the League of Nations mandate to Britain in 1922 – the Jewish Agency – interpreted British obligations as facilitating continued Jewish immigration into Palestine while moving towards an eventual Jewish state in line with the pledge given in the Balfour Declaration of November 1917. The actual wording of both the Balfour Declaration and the terms of mandate was, however, sufficiently vague and contradictory to lead to considerable misunderstanding. In addition successive British governments were increasingly aware of the intractable problems of juggling Jewish and Arab interests in the Middle East. The British moved gradually in the 1930s towards a policy of partition, as recommended by the Peel Commission of 1937, but the difficulties inherent in this solution and the growing Arab discontent with Jewish immigration (as evinced by the 'Arab Revolt' of 1936–39) prompted a reappraisal. This was outlined in the Macdonald White Paper of May 1939. Going some way to meet Arab demands, the government now proposed a limit on Jewish immigration of 750,000 between 1939 and 1944 (when it would cease altogether) and a ten-year transition period to an independent state with an Arab majority. The Jewish Agency believed this to be a clear breach of past pledges but the outbreak of war in Europe in September 1939 saw the acknowledged Jewish leader, David Ben-Gurion, expressing full support for Britain's struggle against Hitler.

During the course of the Second World War, therefore, Britain received assistance from a number of Jewish organisations, including the military arm of the Jewish Agency, the *Haganah* ('Defence'). The Haganah had been formed in January 1920 as an offshoot of the *Histradut*

Below: The progress of Jewish settlement in Palestine was slow until after the First World War, despite the zeal of Theodore Herzl (inset), the 19th-century Zionist leader.

The Jewish population of Palestine

LEBANON

24% Jews as a % of subdistrict population in 1931

● main centres of Jewish population in 1944

MEDITERRANEAN SEA

9%
Safad
1%
29%
Haifa
Tiberias
24%
11%
13%
1%
48%
Tel Aviv Jaffa
12%
41%
Jerusalem
1%
1%

Jews as a percentage of the total population of Palestine 1845-1945

1845   7   11   16   28   31
1914 1922 1931 1936 1945

('General Labour Federation') as a militia to protect Jewish settlements in communal riots. Although the bulk of the Haganah comprised the HIM or territorial force, there was a small field force element (HISH) available for operations. The British Army also received assistance, particularly in the campaign against the Vichy French authorities in Syria in 1941, from the *Palmach* (from *Plugoth Mahatz* or 'Shock Companies'). This had been formed to help defend Palestine against possible German or Italian invasion should the Axis powers overrun British forces in Egypt and it was successor to the 'Special Night Squads' originally formed by Orde Wingate in 1938 to protect the Iraq–Haifa oil pipeline during the Arab Revolt. If the British attitude towards the Haganah and Palmach (who enjoyed a somewhat dubious legality) was rather ambivalent, it was even more so towards a third group which offered help – the *Irgun Zvai Leumi* ('National Military Organisation') or ETZEL.

The Irgun

Originally the name for the non-socialist faction within the Haganah in the early 1930s which favoured the force as a whole remaining a militia rather than becoming the basis for some future national army, the Irgun had been revived in 1937 as the military arm of the New Zionist Organisation. The latter was dedicated to undertaking retaliatory action against the Arabs, but in a way regarded by the Jewish Agency as 'marring the record of Palestine Jewry'. The British authorities could not tolerate Jewish counter-terror even in the midst of the Arab Revolt and the Irgun drifted inexorably into anti-British operations, killing its first policeman in May 1939. Nevertheless, the outbreak of war saw the Irgun, too, ready to declare a temporary truce and its military leader,

Above left: British police in action against anti-Jewish Arab rioters in Jaffa.
Above: A female Haganah member with a home-made Sten gun. Below: Members of the British RAF regiment under attack.

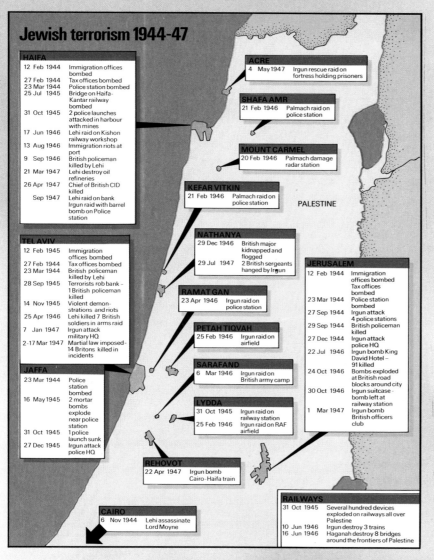

Jewish terrorism 1944-47

HAIFA

12 Feb 1944	Immigration offices bombed
27 Feb 1944	Tax offices bombed
23 Mar 1944	Police station bombed
25 Jul 1945	Bridge on Haifa-Kantar railway bombed
31 Oct 1945	2 police launches attacked in harbour with mines
17 Jun 1946	Lehi raid on Kishon railway workshop
13 Aug 1946	Immigration riots at port
9 Sep 1946	British policeman killed by Lehi
21 Mar 1947	Lehi destroy oil refineries
26 Apr 1947	Chief of British CID killed
Sep 1947	Lehi raid on bank Irgun raid with barrel bomb on Police station

TEL AVIV

12 Feb 1945	Immigration offices bombed
27 Feb 1944	Tax offices bombed
23 Mar 1944	British policeman killed by Lehi
28 Sep 1945	Terrorists rob bank – 1 British policeman killed
14 Nov 1945	Violent demonstrations and riots
25 Apr 1946	Lehi killed 7 British soldiers in arms raid
7 Jan 1947	Irgun attack military HQ
2-17 Mar 1947	Martial law imposed – 14 Britons killed in incidents

JAFFA

23 Mar 1944	Police station bombed
16 May 1945	2 mortar bombs explode near police station
31 Oct 1945	1 police launch sunk
27 Dec 1945	Irgun attack police HQ

REHOVOT

22 Apr 1947	Irgun bomb Cairo-Haifa train

CAIRO

6 Nov 1944	Lehi assassinate Lord Moyne

ACRE

4 May 1947	Irgun rescue raid on fortress holding prisoners

SHAFA AMR

21 Feb 1946	Palmach raid on police station

MOUNT CARMEL

20 Feb 1946	Palmach damage radar station

KEFAR VITKIN

21 Feb 1946	Palmach raid on police station

PALESTINE

NATHANYA

29 Dec 1946	British major kidnapped and flogged
29 Jul 1947	2 British sergeants hanged by Irgun

RAMAT GAN

23 Apr 1946	Irgun raid on police station

PETAH TIQVAH

25 Feb 1946	Irgun raid on airfield

SARAFAND

6 Mar 1946	Irgun raid on British army camp

LYDDA

31 Oct 1945	Irgun raid on railway station
25 Feb 1946	Irgun raid on RAF airfield

JERUSALEM

12 Feb 1944	Immigration offices bombed Tax offices bombed
23 Mar 1944	Police station bombed
27 Sep 1944	Irgun attack 4 police stations
29 Sep 1944	British policeman killed
27 Dec 1944	Irgun attack police HQ
22 Jul 1946	Irgun bomb King David Hotel – 91 killed
24 Oct 1946	Bombs exploded at British road blocks around city
30 Oct 1946	Irgun suitcase-bomb left at railway station
1 Mar 1947	Irgun bomb British officers club

RAILWAYS

31 Oct 1945	Several hundred devices exploded on railways all over Palestine
10 Jun 1946	Irgun destroy 3 trains
16 Jun 1946	Haganah destroy 8 bridges around the frontiers of Palestine

Above: Two of the most determined exponents of Jewish terrorism, Moshe Barazani of LEHI and Meir Feinstein of the Irgun, pictured soon after their arrest. They blew themselves to death with a grenade smuggled into their cell. Left: The progress of Jewish terrorism that made the British mandate impossible. Below: The result of a bomb explosion in Jerusalem.

David Raziel, was killed when his vehicle was bombed by a German aircraft while he was on a mission for the British inside Iraq in May 1941.

There were, however, some members of the Irgun who regarded Britain as a far greater enemy than Hitler and they had broken away under the leadership of Avraham Stern in 1940 to form *Lohamei Heruth Israel* ('Fighters for the Freedom of Israel') or LEHI. Stern was a true revolutionary, prepared to try and enlist the assistance of both Arabs and the Axis powers in an anti-imperialist front against the British. At the same time his vision extended to some kind of Hebrew empire stretching from the Euphrates to the Nile. LEHI, or the 'Stern Gang' as it was more popularly known, began operations against the British authorities in the

autumn of 1940. Its chronic lack of funds and weapons (which forced it into a series of bank raids) and its philosophy of indiscriminate terror deprived Stern of any real popular support and he himself was killed in a police raid in February 1942.

Three months later a Polish Jew, Menachem Begin, arrived in Palestine by way of Russia where he had been a prisoner of war since the Russo-German invasion of Poland in 1939. In 1941 he volunteered for General Anders's Polish Army in Exile and was transferred from the Soviet Union via Iran to Palestine, where he deserted and went into hiding.

Begin's strategy

Like Stern, Begin regarded Britain as the main enemy but in the sense that by deliberately denying Jews a home in their own land of Palestine Britain was conniving at the Nazi extermination policies which were by now becoming evident. Assuming command of the Irgun in December 1943, Begin denounced its truce with Britain in a 'declaration of war' on 1 February 1944. Convinced that Britain could never seriously contemplate outright repression in Palestine, Begin aimed to exert so much pressure through selective terrorism that the British would eventually be faced with a straight choice between total repression or total withdrawal. It was a strategy that has been described as one of 'leverage'. At first, therefore, the Irgun refrained from attacks on military targets while the British were at war with Germany, but this did not preclude attacks on the police or symbolic targets such as immigration offices.

Terrorism in Palestine by the Irgun and LEHI, which mounted a series of revenge attacks after Stern's death, was by no means welcome to the Jewish Agency. As a result, when the Stern Gang assassinated the British Minister Resident in Cairo, Lord Moyne, in November 1944, the Haganah and Palmach were ordered to neutralise the terrorists. The so-called 'Season', during which the Haganah and Palmach 'interned' (and even handed over to the British) Irgun and LEHI members, continued until June 1945 and caused considerable

bitterness in the Jewish community. In fact Moyne's murder had damaged the Jewish cause in precisely the way the Jewish Agency had feared. The British prime minister, Winston Churchill, was far more sympathetic to Jewish aspirations than any of his predecessors. Despite opposition from the Foreign Office, which was always notably pro-Arab, Churchill had pressed for the revival of the pre-war partition plan. During the course of 1943 a Cabinet committee had agreed on such a plan and Churchill was actually having fruitful discussions with Chaim Weizmann of the World Zionist Organisation only two days before the assassination of Moyne, who was a personal friend of the prime minister. As a result, discussion of the partition plan was postponed for the duration of the war.

When the British Labour Party, traditionally a friend of Zionism, entered office in July 1945 there were great expectations on the part of the Jewish Agency that partition and independence would follow shortly, especially as the new American president, Harry Truman, was also favourable to the creation of a Jewish state. These hopes were soon dashed. A number of considerations motivated the policy of the new British Foreign Secretary, Ernest Bevin. There was a growing belief, endorsed strongly by the Foreign Office, that long-term British interests might be better served by concessions to Arabs rather than to Jews. The pledges given to the Arabs to limit Jewish immigration in the 1939 White Paper had already been broken, and

The King David Hotel (main entrance shown below) was the social and administrative centre of the British mandate. But it became a prime target for the extremist Jewish groups and the south-west wing was the victim of a bombing attack in July 1946– with results shown above.

Right: The attack on the King David Hotel shook British, and world, opinion. That the guerrillas could strike with impunity in central Jerusalem seemed a terrible indictment of the failure of British security. The operation was mounted with great care; terrorists smuggled the milk churns in through the main entrance, capturing or shooting all who suspected them, but the messages warning the personnel to evacuate the south-west wing were ignored, partly because the diversionary bombs were thought to have been the main attack.

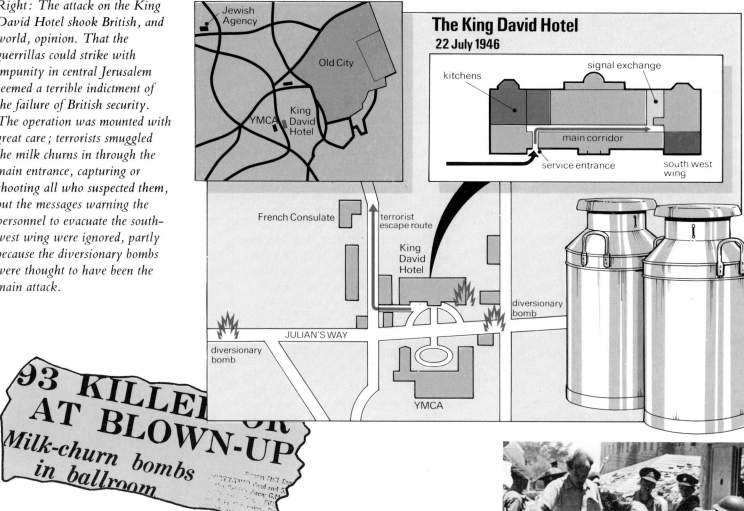

Jewish Agency

Old City

YMCA King David Hotel

The King David Hotel
22 July 1946

kitchens

signal exchange

main corridor

service entrance

south west wing

French Consulate

terrorist escape route

King David Hotel

JULIAN'S WAY

diversionary bomb

diversionary bomb

YMCA

93 KILLED OR AT BLOWN-UP
Milk-churn bombs in ballroom

Truman and the Jewish Agency were now pressing for a further 100,000 European Jews to be immediately admitted. Oil supplies were beginning to be a factor in the government's calculations at a time of British economic weakness and there was also a belief that continued British presence in Palestine could provide a possible Middle East base should Britain be forced to quit Egypt or, at least, a strategic outpost on the route to India. When in November 1945 Bevin announced, in effect, that the White Paper policy of 1939 would be continued, and subsequently remarked that Britain was committed only to a Jewish 'home' in Palestine and not a Jewish state, the patience of the Jewish Agency was finally exhausted.

United Resistance

In August 1945 the British Colonial Office had already refused to allow the quota of Jewish immigrants to be raised and by October the likely shape of Bevin's policy was becoming clear. Little comfort was taken in Bevin's attempt to involve the United States in a joint commission to investigate the Palestinian problem. The Agency therefore patched up its differences with the Irgun and LEHI in the *Tenuat Hameri* ('United Resistance Movement') which also served to provide the Agency with at least a degree of central control. But the participation of the Haganah and Palmach was to be strictly limited to operations loosely designed to facilitate further illegal immigration. Thus, when the joint campaign was launched on the night of 31 October/1 November 1945, the Palmach sank two police launches at Haifa and one at Jaffa while the Haganah attacked the railway system. The nature of Irgun and LEHI participation in the campaign was demonstrated on 27 December by their joint raid on the Jerusalem

and Jaffa CID (Criminal Investigation Department) buildings and a REME (Royal Electrical and Mechanical Engineers) workshop in Tel Aviv, which left 10 British personnel killed and 12 wounded. In fact the Haganah and Palmach mounted only eight operations during the entire period of 'cooperation' and no joint ones after the first night. The Agency continued to agonise over the activities of its partners, for which the British clearly regarded the Agency as responsible. Thus the mounting terrorist campaign prompted major British raids against the Agency and Haganah in Operation Agatha

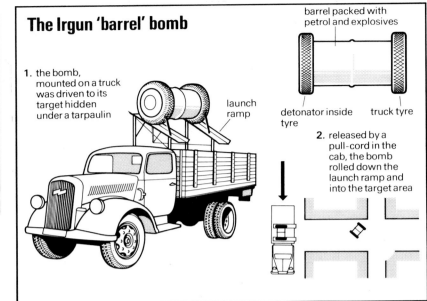

The Irgun 'barrel' bomb

1. the bomb, mounted on a truck was driven to its target hidden under a tarpaulin

launch ramp

barrel packed with petrol and explosives

detonator inside tyre

truck tyre

2. released by a pull-cord in the cab, the bomb rolled down the launch ramp and into the target area

(known to the Jews as 'Black Saturday') on 29 June 1946 and this continued until 1 July. Possibly because of the capture of incriminating documents by the British in the raids, the joint command authorised retaliation in the form of the Irgun's long-planned bombing of the King David Hotel in Jerusalem, part of which housed the British Secretariat in Palestine. On 22 July 1946 seven milk churns packed with explosives demolished the building at a cost of 91 dead and 45 injured. The extent of the casualties finally broke the Agency's resolve and the United Resistance Movement was formally dissolved on 23 August with Haganah and Palmach units ceasing to seek open conflict with the British forces. The Agency also abandoned the World Zionist Organisation's 1942 'Biltmore programme' (which demanded a Jewish state which would include all of Palestine) in favour of some form of partition.

Terror and reprisals

The withdrawal of the Haganah and Palmach, with a potential total strength of some 45,000 members, left the campaign in the hands of an unfettered Irgun, numbering some 1500 activists organised into squads, and LEHI, which numbered barely 300, organised into small cells. Whereas the Agency had always spoken of 'struggle', the Irgun and LEHI spoke of 'war'. Over 58% of all terrorist attacks were now aimed at British personnel, both military and police. The usual methods of attack on personnel were by taxi or truck bombs, which was favoured by LEHI, or by road mines, for which the Irgun developed a particular penchant. On one notable occasion in September 1947 the Irgun also used a 'barrel bomb' – 270kg (600lb) of high explosive packed in a steel drum, driven on a lorry and launched to roll down a ramp into the Haifa police headquarters. In all, just under two-thirds of terrorist attacks were with mines and just under a quarter with bombs.

Supplementing the more general attacks on personnel – such as LEHI's Tel Aviv car-park attack on the night of 25 April 1946, which killed seven members of the British 6th Airborne Division – there were particular efforts aimed at intelligence personnel. Subsidiary operations were mounted on economic targets, such as the LEHI raid on Shell Oil's Haifa refinery on the night of 30 March 1947. However, the next largest single category of attack after personnel – the railways – accounted for only 18% of total attacks. In addition British measures against terrorists were invariably followed by specific reprisals, usually in the form of hostage-taking. After two Irgun members were punished by 18 strokes of the cane, for example, a British major and three NCOs were abducted in December 1946 and flogged. Similarly, a businessman and a judge were kidnapped in January 1947 after the death sentence was passed on another Irgun member, although both men were subsequently released unharmed. The spectacular raid on Acre prison on 4 May 1947, which freed 41 Jewish terrorists and large num-

Opposite below: Frantic attempts to clear a way to the King David Hotel. Above left: The bodies of Martin and Paice hanging in the eucalyptus grove. Above: The 'barrel' bomb, a weapon used to roll explosives over the wire of British security establishments.

bers of Arabs, was a reaction to the execution of four terrorists. In the most notorious incident of all, Sergeants Clifford Martin and Mervyn Paice of the British Field Security Police were kidnapped by the Irgun on 12 July 1947 in retaliation for death sentences passed on three terrorists. Following the execution of the terrorists, the booby-trapped bodies of the sergeants were found hanging from a tree near Nathanya on 31 July.

All terrorist activity was also accompanied by a highly efficient propaganda machine with Irgun and LEHI outlets not only in Palestine but also the United States. The virulently anti-British play 'A Flag is Born', by Ben Hecht, was immensely successful in the United States and both terrorist groups maintained a number of 'fronts' there such as the Irgun's 'American League for a Free Palestine' and LEHI's 'Political Action Committee for Palestine' which raised cash and support. On one occasion an American journalist accused British troops of shooting 20 children in Tel Aviv while singing the *Hörst Wessel* song! The campaign was also briefly (if unsuccessfully) exported in the form of the

Left: A young guerrilla mans a checkpoint with a German Mauser 7.63mm pistol.
Above: A woman Haganah fighter armed with an Austrian 9mm Steyr M12 pistol.
Below: British troops survey the haul of Jewish arms after the security sweeps of 'Black Saturday'.

bombing of the British Embassy in Rome in October 1946 and the attempted bombing of the Colonial Office in London in April 1947. There were a number of attacks on British personnel in Germany and Austria by the Irgun, and LEHI planned but failed to kill Bevin.

British policy

The British response to terrorism in Palestine has been described as that of a 'police state with a conscience'. But the self-imposed restraint of the British, when added to the existing shortcomings

of the coercive machinery available, was hardly conducive to success. The uncertain state of British intentions also lost them the benefits of popular cooperation. The frequent capitulation to terrorist intimidation – although 12 Jews were executed, at least 22 had death sentences commuted under the duress of hostage-taking by April 1947 – equally suggested weakness and a lack of commitment. It was indeed only after the floggings of December 1946 that the government was induced to consider stronger measures. However, when martial law was finally imposed in Tel Aviv and parts of Jerusalem in March 1947 it had already been announced that Britain had decided to turn over the Palestine problem to the United Nations. The imposition of martial law lasted less than three weeks, though it was briefly reimposed in Nathanya in July 1947 after the Martin and Paice murders.

While policy was uncertain, the resources available were far from adequate for the task. Although British forces had faced a politically motivated underground terrorist opponent before – in Ireland between 1919 and 1921 – there was a fatal tendency to treat the situation in Palestine as merely another instance of imperial policing, much like the pre-war Arab Revolt. The problem was that the Palestine Police, although numbering some 20,000 in all, was chronically understrength, especially in British personnel. As a para-military force commanded by and composed primarily of seconded or former British soldiers, it also enjoyed a poor relationship with the local population. Less than 4% of the British personnel spoke Hebrew, while the overwhelming majority of non-British personnel in the regular police were Arab, and the Jewish component was unreliable. The lack of intelligence became so acute that the police were forced to experiment in April 1947 with the ill-fated covert special counter-terrorist squads which led to the highly publicised 'Farran Case'. Roy Farran, a young British war hero who led the squads, was accused of the murder of a LEHI member who had disappeared in May 1947. Farran briefly sought refuge in Syria before returning for trial in October

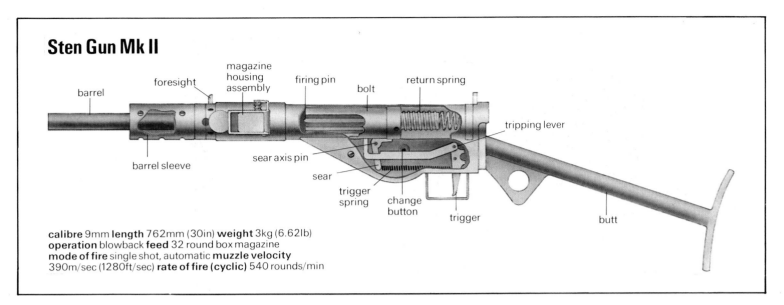

Sten Gun Mk II

barrel
foresight
magazine housing assembly
firing pin
bolt
return spring
tripping lever
barrel sleeve
sear axis pin
sear
trigger spring
change button
trigger
butt

calibre 9mm **length** 762mm (30in) **weight** 3kg (6.62lb)
operation blowback **feed** 32 round box magazine
mode of fire single shot, automatic **muzzle velocity**
390m/sec (1280ft/sec) **rate of fire (cyclic)** 540 rounds/min

1947. He was acquitted for lack of evidence but his brother was subsequently killed in England by a Jewish parcel bomb.

In such circumstances the primary responsibility for counter-insurgency fell to the British Army. The Army's most recent experience, however, had been a major conventional conflict. The 6th Airborne Division, comprising the bulk of the garrison, was regarded as the immediate strategic reserve in the event of a conventional conflict with the Soviet Union in Europe and counter-insurgency seriously interrupted its parachute training. Nor could the Army afford to concentrate entirely on pure counter-insurgency because there was a wide variety of important static points, such as the railways and oil installations, to be guarded, as well as frontier defence and the prevention of illegal immigration. Although some two and a half divisions were eventually deployed – a total of around 90,000 men – the number of troops actually available for offensive operations against the terrorists was quite limited and it was usually a matter of containment. Offensive action that was undertaken mostly consisted of cordon and search operations, usually in response to specific incidents. There were, however, two major operations of this kind – from June to September 1946 in response to the mounting terrorist campaign, and from March to August 1947 in connection with the imposition of martial law and its aftermath. In all over 170 cordon

and search operations were mounted, mostly at battalion or brigade level. In rural areas these would normally consist of an outer cordon of road blocks and armoured patrols and an inner cordon of infantry, while further infantry companies searched the settlements. Urban areas such as Tel Aviv, with a population of over 170,000, represented an altogether greater problem and necessitated an inordinate concentration of force. Operation Agatha, for example – aimed at the Agency and Haganah – involved 10,000 troops and 7000 police in a search of three cities and over 30 settlements, while Operation Shark (30 July to 2 August 1946) involved 21,000 troops imposing a 36-hour curfew on Tel Aviv. Some 787 suspects were detained in the latter case, although the main target, Begin, escaped by hiding in a secret compartment in his house for four days.

Such operations were not always successful and over 25% brought no results at all, but those in March 1947 were generally held to have reduced terrorist activity by over 50%. Cordon and search operations frequently resulted in false accusations being made against troops, so inhabitants had to be required to sign clearance certificates after a search in order to prevent such claims. The strain placed on troops by the many outrages was immense, any reprisals or anti-semitic statements (such as Lieutenant-General Baker's non-fraternisation order after the King David Hotel bombing) being quickly used to brand the British

as 'fascist'. The British were never able to respond successfully to such propaganda, since the press was badly handled and no psychological warfare officers were ever employed in Palestine.

Above: The ubiquitous Sten gun, the most common terrorist weapon. Below: Assembling and arming grenades.

Relinquishing the mandate

In effect the Irgun and LEHI brought the British authorities to the point where a choice had to be made. The Colonial Secretary spoke on 13 February 1947 of the British administration as a 'besieged garrison', and all British women and children were evacuated that month. When the joint British and American Commission had reported in April 1946 it had recommended allowing 100,000 Jewish immigrants to enter Palestine at once and the repeal of all mandate restrictions on Jewish land ownership. This was unacceptable to Britain and Bevin had rejected recommendations he had previously promised to uphold. The involvement of the United States therefore offered no real solution to Britain's problem, while the decision to quit India and the prospect of continued occupation of the Canal Zone had by now robbed Palestine of all strategic significance. Conferences in London having failed in September 1946 and January 1947, Bevin announced on 18 February 1947 that Britain would turn over the problem to the United Nations. A United Nations Special Committee on Palestine (UNSCOP) was established in May. The UN toyed once more with the idea of partition but on 26 September 1947 Britain announced that it would not be responsible for enforcing the UN solution and that it would surrender the mandate and withdraw by 15 May 1948. The campaign had cost 338 British lives (servicemen, police and civilians). In the

remaining months of the British mandate, British security forces were to become involved more in vain efforts to keep the peace than in counter-insurgency, as Jews and Arabs vied for position in what was rapidly turning into a full-scale war.

The Arab response

The Palestinian Arabs had been quiescent during the struggle between the British and the Jewish terrorist groups but this did not mean that they were prepared to allow any form of partition which would establish a separate Jewish state. The vote of the UN Political Committee on 25 November 1947, and that by the General Assembly four days later, to accept the UNSCOP partition plan created such a separate state. (Indeed, Israel remains the

Opposite above: Training with a home-made mortar. The lack of heavy weapons was the main weakness of the Jewish forces as they prepared for the inevitable confrontation with the Arabs in 1948. Opposite below left: Arabs buy weapons and ammunition quite openly on the streets of Jerusalem. The woman is inspecting ammunition to go with her Browning automatic pistol. Opposite below right: Arab irregulars on their way to the fighting on the Mount of Olives, 11 May 1948. Right: The UN Partition plan was an attempt to settle the internecine conflict in Palestine, but it was inevitable that force of arms would decide the boundaries.

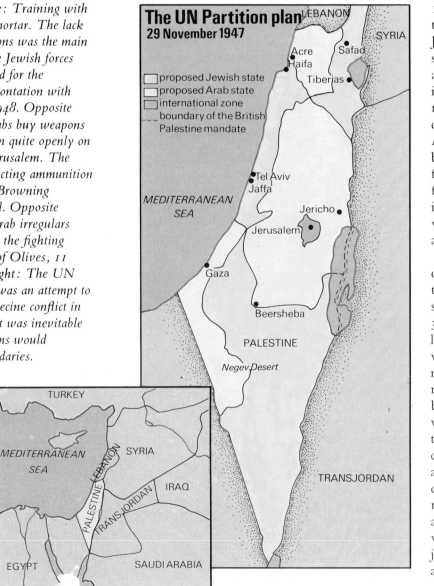

only state to have been created by UN vote.) The vote was met in Palestine by an Arab general strike lasting three days and an immediate outbreak of communal violence. In the first two weeks after the vote, 93 Arabs and 84 Jews died.

The Arabs claimed that Palestine was geographically a part of Syria and that, historically, it was inescapably part of the Arab world. In 1948 the Arabs still outnumbered the Jews in Palestine by two-to-one and owned some 93% of the land, yet the UN intended to go beyond the 1937 partition plan and create a Jewish state of some 500,000 Jews and 450,000 Arabs in three segments which would embrace most of the more productive areas of the country. The Arabs claimed that Palestine should become an independent state by self-determination with

a representative government of all parties, and continued to reject partition. Resistance, however, was hindered by the fact that opposition to a Jewish state was almost the only factor which united the Arabs.

Among the members of the Arab League (formed in March 1945 by Egypt, Syria, Lebanon, Iraq, Saudi Arabia and Transjordan) there were deep divisions. The Syrians claimed Palestine for themselves, while Egypt coveted the Gaza Strip; Lebanon and Iraq were not without their own ambitions. All were highly suspicious of King Abdullah of Transjordan whose proposed 'Greater Syria' under the Hashemite dynasty they had rejected in 1941. Within Palestine itself there were similar rivalries under the nominal control of the Arab Higher Committee which had existed between 1936 and 1937 and had been revived under the leadership of Haj Amin, Mufti of Jerusalem, in 1945. The Mufti, who had spent most of the Second World War as an honoured guest of Nazi Germany, was involved in his own struggle against a rival family faction. He also opposed the direct involvement of the neighbouring Arab states and it was agreed in December 1947 that assistance should be in the form of weapons and 'volunteers'. Therefore, although total Arab military strength in Palestine was over 25,000 men, it was riven by the same kind of factionalism as the Arab world as a whole.

The principal group of some 5000 men operating around Jerusalem was led by the Mufti's cousin, Abdel Kader el Husseini. Another group of approximately 3000 men operating in the Jaffa area was led by the Nazi-trained Hassan Salameh while, in January 1948, the grandly named 'Arab Liberation Army' (ALA), recruited in Damascus and Beirut and led by a Lebanese named Fawzi el Kaukji, was committed across the Jordan River in the Nablus area. The Mufti's faction controlled a youth organisation known as the *Futuwa* in the urban areas and this could also provide some manpower. His rivals maintained the similar *Najada*. In addition some 1700 men became available when the British disbanded the Transjordan Frontier Force in January 1948, and the British-trained 4700-strong Arab

Left: Abdel Kader's forces in the hills above the road to Jerusalem; their attempts to cut off the Jewish community in the Old City led to some of the hardest, and most vicious fighting in the period before the final British withdrawal.

Legion, still nominally part of the British forces, was also keen to join the fray against the Jewish population. Because of the variety of Arab groups involved, there was never any real coordination but, in so far as it existed, the Arab 'strategy' aimed at attacking isolated Jewish settlements, particularly the 33 inside the areas allocated to the Arabs, and at interdicting the routes connecting the three Jewish segments which constituted the proposed Jewish state in the UNSCOP plan.

Battle for Jerusalem

Poorly coordinated though the Arabs were, they still posed a major threat to the Jewish state, especially as they were plentifully supplied with rifles which far outdistanced the pistols and Sten guns generally available for the protection of Jewish convoys on the roads. Ben-Gurion was adamant that no Jewish settlements should be evacuated under any circumstances, even if they were outside Jewish-allocated areas. The 'battle of the roads' therefore assumed prime importance. The Haganah, however, had no experience of major operations and was not suitably organised for them, apart from the HISH component of 4600 and the Palmach of 3000 men (although the British-raised Jewish Settlement Police could provide a further 1800).

The main Jewish problem was the chronic shortage of weapons. In December 1947 there were only 17,000 rifles, some 900 assorted machine-guns and 700 mortars. There were no artillery or anti-tank weapons beyond a few hand-held PIATs. The majority of the Haganah

could only be mobilised slowly and by moral persuasion since no state as yet existed, although by February 1948 it had mustered six brigades and the Palmach had formed ten battalions. There was also the question of integrating the Irgun and LEHI. The defence of the Old City of Jerusalem, for example, was bedevilled by rivalries which the nominal commander, David Shaltiel of the Haganah, could do little to resolve in view of his close association with the 'Season' – the period in 1944–45 when the Jewish Agency had opposed the Irgun and LEHI. The Haganah also had to contend with the continued British presence and frequent arms searches. After an incident in February 1948 when four Haganah members were arrested by the British, disarmed and turned loose in an Arab quarter of Jerusalem to be butchered by the mob, the Haganah resolved to resist arms confiscations.

The first priority was to reopen the roads into Jerusalem, a city which, although placed under international control in the partition plan, was regarded by the Jews as an integral part of their state. In particular the 50km (30-mile) stretch of road from Tel Aviv to the city was a key route. It was dominated by several natural features such as the notorious Bab el Wad defile, and Arab sniping and road blocks caused heavy casualties despite the deployment of truck 'dozers' and improvised armoured cars with firing slits. On 24 March 1948, for example, one Jewish convoy lost 19 of its 40 vehicles; on the following day a convoy of 80 vehicles was unable to break through and had to be extracted by British forces. The situation in the Old City of

Jerusalem was becoming extremely difficult for its Jewish defenders, with food and water running low and power supplies interrupted. The Haganah had mostly confined itself to defensive actions, apart from a number of sabotage operations deep into Arab territory (such as the attack on the Sheikh Hussein bridge over the Jordan River in Febuary 1948), but it was now clear that a major effort was required. Ben-Gurion authorised Operation Nachshon, the first above company level, which would involve 1500 men securing a corridor into Jerusalem through which vitally needed supplies could be safely passed. The operation was due to begin on 1 April 1948 but the problems of organisation were immense and it was only the fortuitous arrival of the first arms supplies from Czechoslovakia, secretly flown into a deserted airfield, that enabled it to proceed. The operation commenced finally on the night of 6 April 1948 and lasted until the 15th, allowing three large convoys to reach Jerusalem. There was particularly hard fighting at Kastel to the east of the corridor, during which Abdel Kader el Husseini was killed, and in a subsidiary operation the Irgun and LEHI mounted their own joint attack on the village of Deir Yassin, west of Jerusalem, on 9 April. In all some 250 Arab men, women and children were killed in the village, an attack roundly condemned by the Haganah. There were, of course, many brutalities on both sides, such as the Arab massacre of the 'Hadassah' hospital convoy in April. But the partial relief of Jerusalem and a reverse for the ALA at Mishmar Haemek had marked a turning point; the Jews now took the offensive.

Top: The call to arms. Haganah forces have just captured this village, and from a hastily improvised strongpoint on the flat roof of a house are replying to fire from an Arab Legion detachment in the next settlement. Above: A Jewish doctor gives first aid during the fighting against Arab forces in Jaffa.

The Palestinian exodus

The main object of this offensive was to gain control of all areas of Palestine designated as part of the Jewish state by the UN, as the British forces withdrew. In the north, Tiberias was taken on 18 April and, as the British left Haifa, the pre-planned Operation Misparayim was implemented to secure immediate control on 22 April. Rather than surrender, however, the Arab forces evacuated by sea, as did some 60,000 Arab civilians. Partly the result of fear (for which the massacre at Deir Yassin was chiefly responsible), partly design and partly in anticipation of an early return, the Arab exodus from Jewish areas was to reach massive proportions in the last months of the mandate. In all it may have amounted to 300,000 people or two-thirds of the Arab population of the designated Jewish state.

Another major target for the Haganah at the end of April was Lydda (Lod), the only international airport in Palestine, which had been allocated to the Jews. Operation Chamatz commenced on 27 April with the Haganah using its new Czech 20mm Hispano-Suiza guns for the first time. Meanwhile, on 25 April, without any authorisation from the Haganah High Command, the Irgun had advanced into Jaffa. The Haganah had intended to bypass Jaffa, which was wholly allocated to the Arabs, in the course of the Lydda operation, but the Irgun had no such scruples and their attack was only halted by the intervention of British armour and aircraft. Subsequently, however, the Arab population began to flee the city and it surrendered on 11 May as soon as British troops had departed the area.

On the Jerusalem front the Haganah failed to push a large convoy and reinforcements into the city on 20 April, but in Operation Jebusi managed to clear many of the surrounding villages. Another effort – Operation Maccabee from 9 to 16 May – effected a temporary reopening of the Jerusalem road (at great cost) but it was closed once more as the mandate expired. South of the city, the Arab Legion overran the so-called 'Etzion Bloc' on 14 May and massacred its defenders. Nevertheless, as the last hours of the mandate approached, Jewish forces had all but destroyed those of the Palestinian Arabs. Four of the five cities, as well as important parts of Jerusalem, much of Galilee and the Negev were in Jewish hands. It was a considerable achievement.

Rebuffing last-minute American attempts to persuade them to remain longer, British forces completed their withdrawal by 14 May, with the exception of some forces around Haifa. A few hours before the mandate was officially due to end at midnight on 14 May 1948, and in order to avoid clashing with the Sabbath, David Ben-Gurion proclaimed the State of Israel at Tel Aviv's City Museum. That night over 30,000 troops drawn from five different Arab armies invaded Israel.

2. The War of 1948-'49

It was at a meeting in Damascus during the first week of May 1948 that the chiefs of staff of the Arab armies formulated a plan for the invasion of Palestine. The Lebanese Army was to attack from the north, aiming for Nahariya on the coast, while the Syrians planned to take the area of Galilee. The Iraqi Army was to cut the Jewish state in half by pushing across the Jordan River to the south of the Sea of Galilee (Lake Tiberias) and capturing Nathanya on the Mediterranean coast. The Jordanian Arab Legion proposed to take Ramle and the district of Samaria, while the Egyptian Army was to push northwards through Gaza and towards Jerusalem in two columns. All in all, the Arab invasion force numbered approximately 37,000 troops, drawn from the armies of Iraq, Syria, Lebanon, Transjordan and Egypt. In addition, there were two guerrilla forces which owed allegiance to the Mufti of Jerusalem (those of the late Abdel Kader el Husseini around Jerusalem and Hassan Salameh around Jaffa), as well as Fawzi el Kaukji's Arab Liberation Army (ALA), which was detailed as a local defence force around Nablus.

The Arab Legion

The strongest of the Arab armies was undoubtedly that of King Abdullah of Jordan, and for that reason he was appointed commander-in-chief of the Arab force. His Arab Legion, commanded by Lieutenant-General Sir John Bagot Glubb (popularly known as 'Glubb Pasha') numbered 10,000 British-trained troops with artillery and armour support.

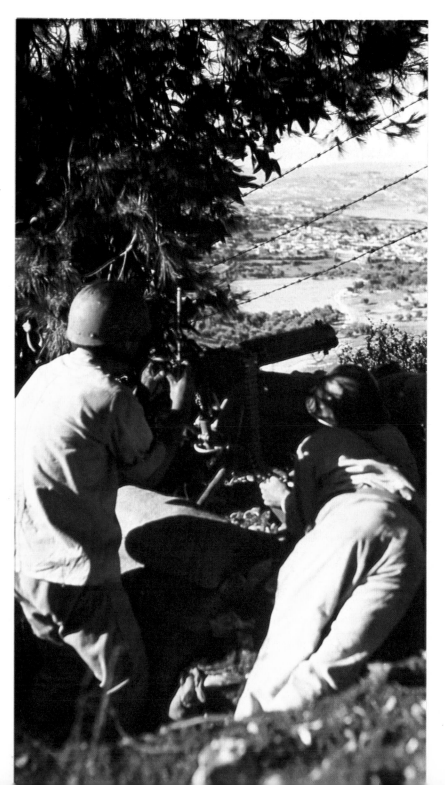

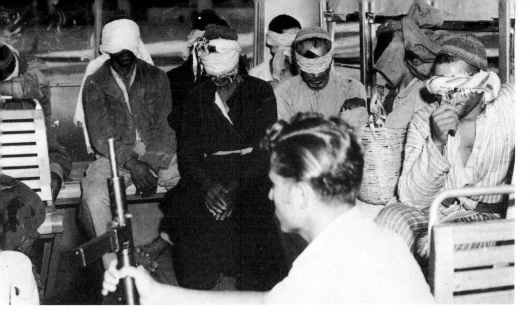

Opposite: Israeli machine-gunners train their water-cooled Vickers Mark 1 on Arab positions in north Palestine, waiting for the assault that their enemies hoped would destroy the fledgling state. Left: Guarded by a Haganah member armed with a Sten gun, blindfolded Arab prisoners are driven away to be interrogated.

However, each Arab army maintained its independent command structure and King Abdullah was unable to impose the coordination that was needed. The five armies may have been well-equipped – all had artillery units, Egypt and Syria had tanks, and Egypt, Syria and Iraq enjoyed air support – but a lack of unity and an underlying distrust of Jordanian motives weakened their impact.

Nevertheless, the Arabs enjoyed a major strategic advantage in that their attacks, even if not executed simultaneously, would cause the Israeli Defence Force (IDF) to fight on three fronts. This was important because, although the IDF was highly mobile and had access to good interior lines of communication, it was ill-equipped and relatively inexperienced. With an effective field force of about 28,000 troops (approximately 12,000 more were available as local Militia), the IDF relied on small-arms, 195 3-inch mortars, some Hispano-Suiza 20mm guns, a few French 65mm howitzers, a number of scout cars and some Czech-built Messerschmitt fighter aircraft that had been acquired in Europe – although the latter had not yet arrived. Thus, when the confrontation between Arab and Jew escalated into open war with the withdrawal of the British on 14 May 1948, the scene appeared to be set for an Israeli tragedy.

The Syrians strike

The attack emerged initially in the north, when Syrian and Lebanese formations moved against a battalion of the Jewish 'Golani' Brigade in the Upper Jordan Valley. The Syrian forces opened the offensive on 14 May with a concentrated artillery bombardment of the Ein Gev area (to the east of the Sea of Galilee) and this was followed up with an armoured advance further south, through Zemach and on towards the Degania villages. At dawn on the 20th the Arabs attacked the Degania villages with a heavy artillery barrage, followed by an infantry advance with armour support. The advance reached the Israeli trenches, but the defenders, using Molotov cocktails and PIAT anti-tank weapons, managed to repulse the Syrians – mainly because the bulk of their infantry had not kept up with the armoured spearhead.

Later in the day a second Syrian advance proved to be no more successful, and it was at this point that the Israelis suddenly seized the initiative. Artillery pieces that had only recently arrived in Tel Aviv were rushed to the north and, with no training whatsoever, the IDF managed to get them into action. A few practice shots were used to zero the guns and it was not long before Israeli shells were hitting Syrian targets. They caused panic among the Syrians who, until this point, had been able to exploit the lack of Israeli hitting power. As the Syrians withdrew, the Israelis advanced to recapture all the territory that had fallen to the invaders. By 23 May the Israelis had effectively cleared the Jordan Valley.

With a characteristic lack of coordination, the main Lebanese attack did not materialise until 6 June, when Malkiya in the western sector of Galilee was suddenly assaulted. The Syrians, having regrouped, used the opportunity to move against Mishmar Hayarden in an attempt to sever the Israeli north–south resupply route in central Galilee. It proved too much for the over-stretched IDF. The Lebanese, with the help of the ALA, quickly took Malkiya, followed this up with the capture of Kadesh and linked up with ALA units in central Galilee. In the Mishmar Hayarden sector the Syrian attack was particularly well-coordinated and a two-pronged advance began. Although repulsed once, the Syrians eventually took the town and headed towards the main road. They were blocked by hastily assembled IDF reinforcements just as the first of the United Nations' truces came into effect on 11 June.

Across the Jordan

Meanwhile, in the east, an Iraqi force had forded the Jordan River near Gesher on 15 May. Repulsed by Israeli units in the area, the Iraqis withdrew and moved south, crossing the river towards Nablus. In a concentrated spearhead they advanced through Israel, hoping effectively to bisect the country, and successfully reached to within 12km (8 miles) of Nathanya. On the night of 31 May the Israelis, aware of the danger, launched a hastily prepared counter-attack. However, the assault failed and the key town of Jenin fell to the Iraqis.

While this was going on, the Arab Legion advanced on Jerusalem and despite hard-fought, close-quarter actions – in which Palmach units excelled themselves – the Jordanians eventually took the Old City on 20 May. This was a major blow to the morale of the IDF

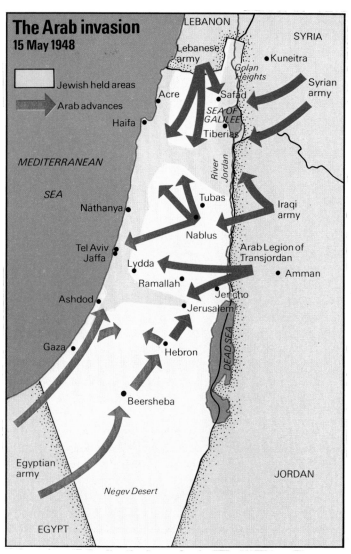

The Arab invasion
15 May 1948

◻ Jewish held areas
➡ Arab advances

LEBANON

Lebanese army

SYRIA

• Kuneitra

Golan Heights

Syrian army

Acre

Safad

SEA OF GALILEE

Haifa •

Tiberias

MEDITERRANEAN

SEA

River Jordan

Nathanya •

Tubas

Iraqi army

Nablus

Tel Aviv
Jaffa

Lydda

Ramallah

Arab Legion of Transjordan

• Amman

Ashdod •

Jericho

Jerusalem

Gaza •

DEAD SEA

Hebron

Beersheba •

JORDAN

Egyptian army

Negev Desert

EGYPT

as the Old City had long been a bastion of Jewish strength and, with its holy shrines (including the Wailing Wall), a symbol of Jewish faith.

On the southern front, the Egyptian advance had also begun on 14 May, when a force of approximately 7000 men crossed into Israel in two separate columns, supported by armour, artillery and air power. While a small brigade group of some 2000 men followed an interior route towards Beersheba, a larger brigade group of 5000 troops pushed along the coast towards Gaza. Despite Egyptian superiority in arms, equipment and numbers – the Israelis could only deploy two brigades, the total strength of which was approximately 3800 men – the advance soon degenerated into a series of stalemates. Scattered Israeli settlements put up fierce resistance and the IDF fought well, exploiting local knowledge and making the most of Egyptian failures to

coordinate their artillery, armour and infantry. To cite just one example, the 30 young defenders of the village of Kfar Darom, to the south of Gaza, managed to hold out against overwhelming Egyptian forces for nearly a month and were only evacuated on direct orders from IDF Command during the UN truce when it was obvious that they could do no more. This and other similar incidents convinced the Egyptians that it would not be prudent to engage each and every settlement along the way.

The first ceasefire

Thus, when the Egyptians resumed their advance on 20 May, they bypassed minor settlements and succeeded in taking the town of Yad Mordechai. But the delays imposed by the local Israeli forces had given the IDF a vital opportunity to build up its strength, particularly in air power.

Above left: The Arab invasion routes. Above: Israeli troops rest after taking Karkoun village. Opposite above: Jewish forces defend a fortified house. At this early stage in the fighting, equipment was still scarce – hence the machine-gun they have is a British Lewis Gun of First World War vintage. Opposite centre: Moshe Dayan who commanded 89th Commando Battalion in 1948. Opposite far right: The human cost. Palestinian Arabs leaving Jewish-held areas.

On 29 May the embryonic Israeli Air Force (IAF), having at last received some fighter planes from Europe, flew its first sorties against the advancing Arab columns. While the strafing attacks were of little practical use, the sudden appearance of Israeli aircraft was enough to induce the Egyptians to halt their advance and concentrate on consolidating their lines of communication, with the aim of completely isolating the Negev sector.

Just before the first truce came into effect on 11 June the Egyptians managed to gain command of the main Majdal (Ashkelon)–Faluja highway and effectively cut off the Negev but, given their initial strength, this was a disappointing outcome to nearly a month's fighting.

The Israelis, under pressure on three fronts, could thus gain some comfort from their achievements during this first phase of the fighting (14 May–11 June). In the north, despite tough battles and the loss of key territory around Kadesh and Mishmar Hayarden, the IDF had not been overwhelmed; in the south a sub-

lead to a permanent settlement were in vain. Both sides regarded it as merely a breathing space in which to consolidate in preparation for the next round of armed conflict. On 9 July 1948, at the end of the 28-day period laid down in the terms of the truce agreement, hostilities were resumed.

The fighting restarts

During the truce, the Syrians had substantially reinforced their bridgehead at Mishmar Hayarden, until it contained an infantry brigade with armour and artil-

lery support, a further brigade holding the Syrian (Golan) Heights overlooking the east bank of the Jordan River. The Lebanese Army, to the north of the Syrian positions, was deployed along a front reaching from Rosh Hanikra to Bint Jbeil near Malkiya. This deployment ensured constant supply and reinforcement routes for Kaukji's ALA in central Galilee. As the truce ended, the Israeli High Command, responsible for the five brigades of the IDF deployed along the northern front, prepared two counter-moves: Operation Brosh ('Cypress Tree'), aimed at encircling and isolating the Syrians at Mishmar Hayarden, and Operation Dekel ('Palm Tree'), to destroy the weakest link in the Arab chain – the ALA.

During the night of 9/10 July the 'Carmeli' Brigade, supported by the newly raised 'Oded' Brigade, launched the encircling offensive against the Syrian bridgehead. Although one battalion managed to cross the Jordan River, heavy fire from Syrian artillery prevented engineers from erecting a pontoon bridge. At the same time, word was received that the Syrians were planning to launch an assault in the direction of Rosh Pinah. With daylight approaching, only one battalion across the Jordan and under

stantial Egyptian assault had been contained. Even so, the overall strategic situation was still worrying, for it was obvious that the Arab threat was not going to disappear, while in the east, where the Iraqis had virtually cut through to the coast at Nathanya and the Jordanians were laying siege to Jerusalem, the very existence of Israel lay precariously in the balance. Because of this, all hopes that the UN truce agreement of 11 June would

The Arab exodus – 1948

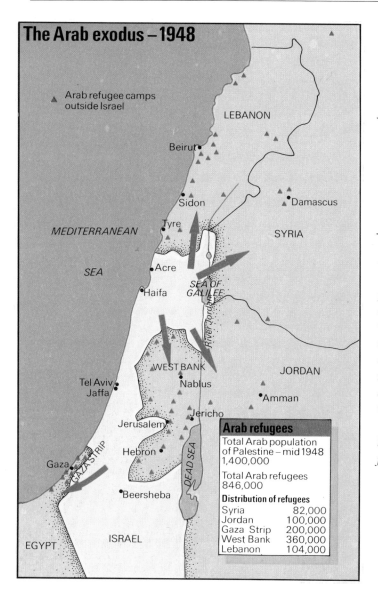

▲ Arab refugee camps outside Israel

LEBANON

Beirut

Sidon

• Damascus

Tyre

MEDITERRANEAN

SYRIA

• Acre

SEA

• Haifa

SEA OF GALILEE

River Jordan

WEST BANK

JORDAN

Tel Aviv •
Jaffa •

• Nablus

• Amman

• Jericho

Jerusalem •

GAZA STRIP

Hebron •

DEAD SEA

Gaza •

• Beersheba

EGYPT

ISRAEL

Arab refugees

Total Arab population of Palestine – mid 1948
1,400,000

Total Arab refugees
846,000

Distribution of refugees

Syria	82,000
Jordan	100,000
Gaza Strip	200,000
West Bank	360,000
Lebanon	104,000

Left: The dispersal of the Palestinian Arabs in 1948. The mutual hostility between Jewish and Arab nationalism was given a further twist by this diaspora. Below: One of Israel's first tanks – a Cromwell stolen from a British base shortly before the final British withdrawal. Bottom: Jewish irregulars defend their village against Arab attack. Opposite above: Guarding an Arab prisoner in a recently taken settlement. Opposite below: An improvised armoured convoy – sheets of metal make a truck into an armoured car, while an ex-German Second World War MG34 'Spandau' has been bolted to the jeep.

on 14 July the ALA launched eight successive offensives backed up with mortar fire and air strikes – the ALA could not defeat the IDF. The appearance at the rear of the ALA forces of the Israeli 7th Brigade, pushing forward towards Nazareth, forced Kaukji to reorganise and send his mobile reserve to engage this new threat. As the Arabs approached, the IDF's only self-propelled 20mm gun in that area engaged the ALA mobile unit at a range of some 500m (550yd) and succeeded in wiping out six of the eight advancing vehicles. By 16 July the Arab force had withdrawn and Nazareth had fallen to the IDF. Thus, by 18 July the ALA had been effectively neutralised as a fighting force and, as the second truce was imposed, it began to retreat to the north-east. The IDF was beginning to bite back.

Operation Danny

Meanwhile, on the eastern front, the Israelis faced their most powerful adversary. The Jordanian Arab Legion was well established on high ground that dominated Lydda (Lod), with its international airport and strategic rail junction and, in the Latrun sector, threatened the vital road linking Tel Aviv and the Jewish enclave in Jerusalem. In addition, Jerusalem itself was under siege. To

constant artillery attack, the Israeli forces were ordered back and the attempt to cut the Syrian supply lines and isolate the bridgehead was called off. At dawn on 10 July the Syrians launched a counter-attack. The Syrian units commanding the heights to the east of the Jordan attacked those units of the IDF that had remained on the eastern bank, while the rest of the Syrian force pushed towards Rosh Pinah. The conflict, though bitter, gained neither side any territory and, after nine days of fighting, when a second UN truce came into operation, both armies occupied almost the same positions as they had initially.

In western Galilee the IDF launched its operation to dislodge the ALA, also on 9 July, concentrating on the village of Sejera. It was here that Kaukji concentrated his forces and despite severe fighting –

towns. But Glubb was not giving in, for while this was going on he was concentrating his Legion troops in the strategically important Latrun sector, threatening the road to Jerusalem. The Israelis initially tried to bypass these positions, clearing the way in attacks launched late on 15 July, but Glubb organised a counter-attack that prevented the loss of the Latrun Ridge. The Israelis launched further offensives which degenerated into some of the bitterest fighting of the 1948 campaign. The results were inconclusive, for although the IDF succeeded in capturing the airport at Lydda and removing the immediate threat to Tel Aviv, the Jordanians still controlled the Jerusalem road.

relieve the situation – the continuance of which could be disastrous for the future of an independent Israel – the IDF planned Operation Danny, designed to occupy Lydda and Ramle, capture Latrun and Ramallah and lift the blockade around Jerusalem. The forces to be used were the 'Yiftach', 'Harel', 'Kiryati' and 8th Armoured Brigades, with support from elements of the 'Etzioni' and 'Alexandroni' Brigades – representing a substantial commitment of scarce resources.

On the night of 9/10 July the Israelis attacked the Arab Legion in Lydda. Glubb, aware that his forces could not hold the town, did not reinforce the garrison and the Israelis quickly gained control. This was immediately followed up by an offensive against Ramle and by the 10th the IDF had captured both

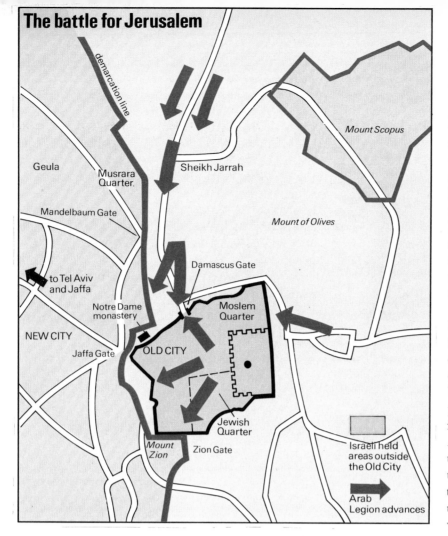

The battle for Jerusalem

demarcation line

Mount Scopus

Geula

Musrara Quarter

Sheikh Jarrah

Mandelbaum Gate

Mount of Olives

to Tel Aviv and Jaffa

Notre Dame monastery

Damascus Gate

Moslem Quarter

NEW CITY

Jaffa Gate

OLD CITY

Mount Zion

Zion Gate

Jewish Quarter

Israeli held areas outside the Old City

Arab Legion advances

Above: The Arab capture of the Old City. Below: Arab Legion soldiers in Jerusalem. Opposite below: Arab Legion Vickers machine-gun crews. Opposite above: A French Hotchkiss machine gun manned by Arab irregulars.

The road to the Negev

Prior to the end of the first truce, the IDF had also prepared plans for offensives against the Egyptians in the south. The aim was to reopen a road into the Negev, so forcing the Egyptians back from Ashdod and cutting their east–west supply route. At the same time, the Egyptians

planned to widen their corridor in order to improve their lines of communication. Having watched the Israeli preparations, the Arabs decided to launch a pre-emptive strike and on 8 July – the day before the truce officially ended – they attacked and captured IDF positions at Kaukaba, Huleiqat and Hill 113. Severe fighting followed, and for five days the Egyptians launched various unsuccessful offensives against Negba and Beerot Yitzhak. By the time the second truce came into effect on 18 July, the IDF had opened a narrow corridor into the Negev.

Once again it was UN pressure that brought about a temporary lull in hostilities. Although both sides probably needed the respite, it undoubtedly favoured the Jews. Their strategic position had begun to improve during this second phase of the war (9–18 July) and they had inflicted morale-boosting defeats on the Arab forces. Israel was still neither victorious nor secure, but with every day that passed the IDF was learning the tricks of its trade. The second truce was used by the Israelis to recuperate, restock with heavy weapons and prepare for yet another, hopefully successful, round of fighting. By comparison the Arabs, suffering the first shocks of defeat at the hands of an enemy that they had seriously underestimated, and lacking the unity of purpose that was so desperately needed, merely licked their wounds.

Thus when the second truce petered out in late October 1948, the IDF High Command felt confident enough to launch a series of offensives designed to rid Israel of the Arab military presence. One of the first priorities was to clear Galilee and carve out a buffer-zone on the northern front. On the night of 28/29 October Operation Hiram, involving four infantry brigades and four batteries of artillery, was launched. The aim was to advance in two pincers which would link up in the town of Sasa, encircling Arab forces in the area.

The eastern arm of the pincer, spearheaded by the Israeli 7th Brigade, encountered little resistance but the 'Oded' Brigade in the west found the going hard. However, once the Arabs realised that the 7th Brigade was in their rear, they began to disengage and, as the IDF kept up the

pressure through a series of supplementary offensives, a withdrawal towards Lebanon quickly developed. The Syrians managed to retain their bridgehead at Mishmar Hayarden but by 31 October, after a campaign which showed many of the characteristics of rudimentary blitzkrieg, the Israelis controlled the whole of Galilee.

Arab withdrawal

On the southern front, Operation Yoav had already begun on 15 October. By means of a large-scale attack, the IDF intended to force open a wide corridor into the Negev, cutting Egyptian lines of communication and forcing the enemy to withdraw. In the early stages of the attack, however, the IDF was easily repulsed, suffering heavy casualties in attempts to take fortified hilltop positions, particularly Hills 113 and 100. But after an initial retreat, and under cover of a heavy artillery barrage, the IDF resumed the offensive. A successful diversionary feint meant that Egyptian troops were caught by surprise when the main attack was launched. By 18 October the Israelis controlled the hilltops and road junctions that dominated the main east–west (Majdal–Hebron) axis. The offensive was followed through with an attack that took Kaukaba to the south. Although efforts to take the key position at Huleiqat and widen the corridor into the Negev met with stiff resistance from the Egyptian Army, further offensives along the coast in the Majdal area threatened the Arabs with encirclement and they began to withdraw steadily southwards using coastal routes.

This withdrawal soon led to bitter inter-Arab disputes as many felt that Egypt's retreat bordered on a betrayal of the common aim – the destruction of the Jewish state. The Israelis, realising that because of this it was unlikely that other Arab armies would come to the aid of the Egyptians, decided to launch an all-out offensive against the Huleiqat stronghold. The attack began on 19 October and the determination of the IDF finally broke the Egyptian stranglehold. Operation Horev, which was virtually a clearing operation aimed at removing the Egyp-

tians from their footholds in Israel, was launched on 22 December and by the 27th Egypt's eastern front in the Negev had given way entirely. The Israelis crossed the border into Sinai and took Abu Aweigila against minimal opposition. The British government then stepped in and presented the Israelis with an ultimatum: unless they withdrew from Egyptian territory immediately, Britain would be forced to come to Egypt's assistance. In the face of such a threat, the Israelis had no choice but to accede and thereafter the IDF turned its attention to Egyptian positions around Rafah in the Gaza area. Egypt, realising the hopelessness of her situation, opened talks that led eventually to the signing of an armistice with Israel on 24 February 1949.

Mobility, surprise and improvisation

By that time a general ceasefire had been arranged, effective from 7 January. An armistice with Lebanon was signed on 23 March and one with Jordan followed 11 days later – after the Israelis had asserted their control of the southern Negev and gained access to the Gulf of Aqaba by entering Um-Rashrash (Elat) unopposed. Syria was the last to sign an armistice, on 20 July. Although she withdrew from Mishmar Hayarden, it was agreed that the bridgehead should be demilitarised. None of the Arab nations acknowledged or accepted the Israeli state, but their defeat at the hands of the IDF ensured the emergence of a Jewish homeland in fact as well as in name.

It is difficult, on the face of it, to understand the overwhelming success of the IDF in the field, considering the enormous disadvantages under which it entered what the Israelis call, with some justification, the 'War of Independence'.

The IDF, compared to the Arab armies, was weak in terms of manpower, lacked modern weapons and was forced to fight on three fronts. But it was these very disadvantages that led to the development of a strategy based on mobility, surprise and improvisation. Nearly all IDF operations, for example, were launched during the hours of darkness to negate the Arab air advantage, and this method of warfare became second nature to the soldiers of the IDF. This contrasted strongly with the rather pedestrian approach of Arab commanders, who consistently showed a lack of initiative, especially in the offensive. Command at a higher level was also suspect – the Arabs, despite their numerical superiority and respectable equipment, were unable to unite in a common strategy or to elect a high command that could ultimately coordinate the combined Arab forces. In the end, it was mutual distrust and a lack of communication among the Arabs that allowed Jewish bravery, resourcefulness and determination to win a notable victory in the War of 1948-49. It was a pattern that was to be repeated.

3. A New Arab World

The results of the War of 1948–49 could not be regarded as either permanent or satisfactory. The five Arab nations involved had been humiliated and forced to surrender territory in Palestine under military pressure, and for these reasons they refused to recognise Israel as an independent sovereign state, even after she had been admitted to the United Nations. This in turn forced Israel to create what was virtually a 'garrison' within her borders, protected by a vigilant IDF which required a constant flow of modern military equipment and access to an enormous pool of reinforcements in times of crisis or war. Money and manpower therefore became the keys to Israeli survival but, despite private and public gifts from around the world (especially the United States), reparations from West Germany and a deliberate policy of attracting maximum immigration, neither could be permanently guaranteed. Indeed, the devotion of so many resources to defence, the influx of unearned money and the arrival of immigrants whose productive (and military) capacity was limited, at least until they had learnt a common language, combined to undermine an already precarious economy and produce a problem of inflation that was soon to become an endemic worry.

Armed confrontation

The security of Israel could not be compromised, however, particularly as the borders carved out in 1948–49, although from the Jewish point of view representing an improvement on the terms of the

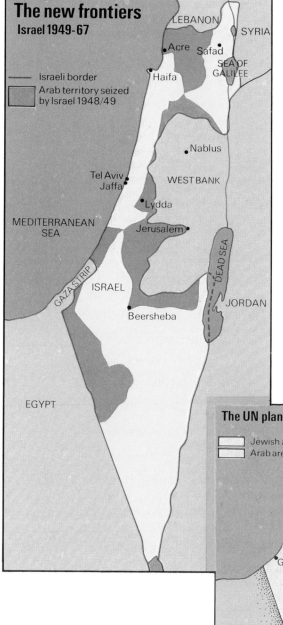

The new frontiers
Israel 1949-67

— Israeli border
▨ Arab territory seized by Israel 1948/49

LEBANON
SYRIA
Acre · Safad
SEA OF GALILEE
Haifa
· Nablus
Tel Aviv · WEST BANK
Jaffa
· Lydda
MEDITERRANEAN SEA
Jerusalem ·
GAZA STRIP
ISRAEL
DEAD SEA
JORDAN
Beersheba
EGYPT

The UN plan

LEBANON
SYRIA
☐ Jewish areas
☐ Arab areas
· Haifa

· Tel Aviv

Jerusalem

· Gaza

· Beersheba
PALESTINE
TRANSJORDAN
EGYPT

UN partition plan of 1947, were extremely vulnerable. In the north, the border with Lebanon was not easy to defend, requiring military forces that could not always be made available in peacetime, while the Syrians continued to hold positions on the Golan Heights, dominating the Galilee plain. In the east, Jordanian troops remained entrenched in the hills of Samaria and Judea (the 'West Bank'), overlooking the thin coastal strip of Israel and occupying positions within a few kilometres of targets such as Tel Aviv, Lydda (Lod) and Nathanya. In addition, the Arab Legion was firmly in possession of key areas of Jerusalem and dug-in on the high ground from Latrun to Ramallah, dominating the road from Tel Aviv. Finally, in the south, the Egyptians were in Sinai and the Gaza Strip, threatening the Negev and its coastal plain, and had the potential to control Israeli access to maritime trading routes through the Straits of Tiran and

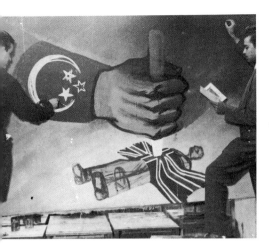

Opposite: The new frontiers established as a result of the 1948–49 war. The Arab defeat had great repercussions, most notably in Egypt, where a wave of revolutionary nationalism was soon to overthrow the old monarchy. Left: An Egyptian puts the finishing touches to an anti-British poster. Right: Anthony Eden, prime minister of Great Britain, had to deal with the problems caused by the delicate issue of the Suez Canal. Below: The Canal was affected by a number of political conflicts, but its strategic position seemed vital to British interests in the eastern Mediterranean.

the Suez Canal. In strategic terms, the Jewish state seemed to be constantly poised on the brink of disaster.

Fortunately for the Israelis, the armistice agreements of 1949 were followed by over seven years of comparative peace. Arab *fedayeen* ('freedom fighters') occasionally crossed the borders to mount hit-and-run attacks, but an all-out Arab assault did not materialise. This was undoubtedly due in part to the deterrent value of the IDF, but there was more to it than that. The defeats of 1948–49 seriously undermined the stability of the Arab world, destroying all hopes of unity or coordination. In Jordan, King Abdullah was assassinated by a Palestinian Arab at the Aqsa Mosque in July 1951; after a brief interlude under his deranged son Talal, his grandson Hussein ascended the throne in 1953. He was to prove to be one of life's 'survivors', but the fate of his grandfather and the knowledge that his army could never defeat Israel on its own, tended to moderate his policy towards his Jewish neighbour. Iraq was to avoid political turmoil for a while, but in Syria the defeat of 1948–49 was followed by a series of military coups that effectively neutralised her status as a 'front-line' state.

In Egypt, the impact of the Arab humiliation was equally profound though, typically, it took longer to mature. The war had produced few heroes and the wrath of the younger generations, especially within the Free Officers' Movement, was aimed at their own High Command which had displayed such incompetence. The results were to be far-reaching, thrusting Egypt firmly to

the fore in the Arab opposition to Israel and contributing to the steady escalation of confrontation that was to lead, inevitably, to yet more conflict.

Nasser takes power

King Farouk of Egypt rapidly lost what little popularity he had in the aftermath of the 1948–49 War and his country soon became ungovernable. An attempt by the Wafd Party to focus national resentment on the continued British presence in Egypt rather than on the ailing monarchy,

failed to relieve the pressure, and on 23 July 1952 the politically radical Free Officers' Movement intervened in a near-bloodless military coup. Farouk was quickly despatched into exile and Egypt's *ancien régime* collapsed.

The nominal Head of State was General Mohammed Neguib, one of the few in the High Command to have distinguished himself in the war with Israel. Real power, however, lay with the tall, silent figure of his prime minister, Gamal Abdel Nasser. In these early days Nasser showed little inclination for the Pan-

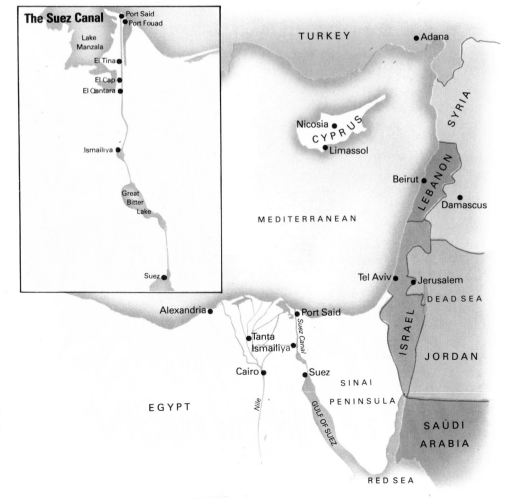

Arab movement – instead he and his fellow military rulers were imbued with a profound sense of Egyptian nationalism. It was a feeling that was to lead to a number of changes: a formal end to the monarchy, reform of the social and economic infrastructure of the state and an insistence that Egypt should be free from outside, predominantly European, influence. When Neguib proved to be too conservative-minded to agree, he was easily outmanoeuvred by Nasser who, by the end of 1954, had emerged as virtual Head of State.

The end of Britain's military presence

Nasser saw Egypt as lying at the centre of the three circles of the African, Arab and Islamic worlds. He was determined that his country should now play its full part in international affairs. First, however, it was necessary to rid the state of the last vestiges of British military presence. This did not prove too difficult, though Nasser was not above using the occasional guerrilla outrage against British forces as a negotiating medium. British Middle East Headquarters had already been moved to Cyprus, which reflected the declining importance of the Canal to Britain after the 'loss' of India in 1947. Washington also pressed London to be 'reasonable', for US Secretary of State John Foster Dulles was anxious to recruit Nasser to the Western cause.

Terms of withdrawal were agreed by July 1954, and the British garrison began its evacuation immediately. On 31 March 1956 the 2nd Battalion, Grenadier Guards and D Squadron, the Life Guards embarked at Port Said and their departure brought 74 years of British military presence to a close. As a result of these moves, Nasser felt able to take a less overtly Western stance, epitomised by his attendance in April 1955 at the Bandung Conference, where he embraced the ideologies of the non-aligned world. He returned to Cairo determined to create a neutral Arab bloc under Egyptian leadership.

Though Naser thus spurned the West, others in the Arab world did not. The Americans were determined to shore up the northern tier of Middle East states as part of their containment of the Soviet Union. Iraq, now ruled by the young Feisal II and guided by his prime minister and grandfather's chief of staff, Nuri Said, became a founder member of the American-sponsored Baghdad Pact in February 1955. Egypt was furious at such a blatant denial of Arab neutralism and Nasser drifted further away from the Western camp. During 1955 he managed to alienate the 'big three' of the Western world one after another. Radio Cairo's propaganda tirades against Iraq angered Dulles; espousal and support for Mau Mau in Kenya and the FLN (*Front de Libération Nationale*) in Algeria in the name of anti-colonialism aroused the anger of Britain and France.

It is against this background that Israeli foreign policy in the early 1950s must be viewed. One of her first priorities was the search for sympathetic allies from whom she could purchase modern military equipment, and it was during this process that she came into close contact with the French. In August 1954 influential men from the military establishments of both countries met and soon realised that they had a common enemy in the person of President Nasser. His support for Arab nationalism in Morocco, Tunisia and Algeria guaranteed the opposition of France; his intransigence over demands for navigation rights in the Gulf of Aqaba and his refusal to curb the actions of Palestinian refugees in the Gaza Strip angered the Israelis. This common ground was manifested initially in secret French arms deals with Israel, but by June 1955 the two countries began discussing the possibility of concerted military action against the Cairo regime. Some weeks later, Israel's prime minister, David Ben-Gurion, warned Egypt that he would fight to open the Gulf of Aqaba if Nasser ever tried to deny passage to Israeli ships.

Cross-border raids

Nor was this the full extent of Israeli action, for as cross-border *fedayeen* raids intensified, she proved both willing and able to retaliate, sending IDF units to attack Palestinian camps and Egyptian military positions in the Gaza Strip. On 28 February 1955, for example, two platoons of Israeli paratroopers infiltrated across the Armistice Line and attacked an Egyptian Army post actually in the town

of Gaza. They withdrew after a three-hour firefight in which buildings, equipment and installations were destroyed and over 20 Egyptian soldiers killed. Later in the year, a similar strike was made against an Egyptian police post at Khan Yunis, to the south of Gaza and, on 21 September, the demilitarised zone at Al Auja was occupied.

Nasser realised that his army was in desperate need of modernisation and, despite his declared policy of neutralism, he had no choice but to seek outside aid. At first he tried to purchase the weapons he needed from Britain and the United States, but they refused, citing an international agreement of 1950 by which they, together with France, had declared that all arms deliveries to the Middle East were to maintain a rough parity

Opposite left: Gamal Abdel Nasser in 1953, just before he replaced Neguib as leader of Egypt. Opposite right: Nasser's dream – the Aswan Dam under construction. Funding the Dam was one of the main motives behind nationalising the Suez Canal. Above right: British troops leave Port Said, evacuating the Canal Zone. Below: British domestic opinion was not all belligerent as tension mounted in 1956. Above: HMS Theseus prepares to sail to the Mediterranean from Portsmouth.

between Israel and the Arabs. France, of course, had already broken this agreement through her arms deal with Israel alone, but neither Britain nor the United States seems to have been aware of this at the time.

The Aswan High Dam

In an attempt to force British and American hands, Nasser let it be known that he intended to approach the Soviet Union instead, and when this failed to have the desired effect, he went ahead. On 27 September 1955, in the immediate aftermath of the Israeli attack on Al Auja, Nasser signed an arms deal, sponsored by the Soviets, with Czechoslovakia. In exchange for cotton, the Czechs agreed to supply 530 armoured vehicles, about 500 artillery pieces and up to 200 combat aircraft, all from stocks which the Soviets swiftly replaced. The French responded by stepping up supplies of the Mystère IV jet fighter and AMX-13 light tank to Israel. An arms race – the inevitable prelude to renewed conflict – began.

Both Britain and the United States tried to play down the significance of Nasser's new deal and, for a time, they followed a

Daily Mirror
TUES AUG. 14 1956
2ᴰ FORWARD WITH THE PEOPLE
No. 16,383

The 'Mirror's' Message to Eden

NO WAR OVER EGYPT!

THE 24-Power Conference on the Suez Canal is now going to be a 22-Power Conference. It opens in London on Thursday—with Egypt and Greece absent and with Russia ominously present.

Opposite inset: Cheering crowds greet Nasser on the announcement that the Suez Canal had been nationalised. Anglo-French reaction was to seek a military solution, and planning began for Operation Musketeer (right) which was to follow an Israeli attack in Sinai. Opposite below: Paratroops bound for Egypt emplane in Cyprus. The assembling of the forces for the invasion of Egypt was a considerable feat.

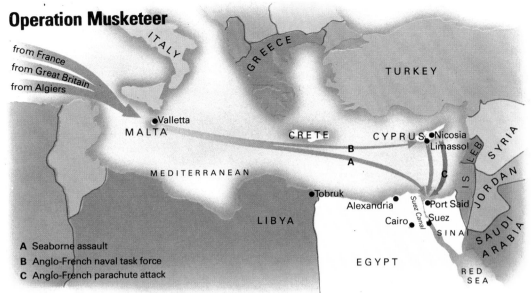

Operation Musketeer

from France
from Great Britain
from Algiers

A Seaborne assault
B Anglo-French naval task force
C Anglo-French parachute attack

conciliatory line towards the Egyptian leader, particularly over the negotiation of loans to finance the important Aswan High Dam project. This was to be the 'pyramid' of the new Egypt, designed to revitalise the country's economy, irrigate the land and provide hydro-electric power in areas otherwise starved of natural energy resources. It was Nasser's dream and he looked to the Western powers for the financial assistance he needed. To begin with, they agreed, organising one loan which was to be Anglo-American and another from the World Bank, but as events unfolded in the Middle East, the prospects of such support began to diminish.

The British government, headed by Sir Anthony Eden, blamed Nasser for a steady deterioration in Anglo-Arab relations, epitomised by the growing opposition to the Baghdad Pact and, more especially, the dismissal of 'Glubb Pasha' from his command of the Jordanian Arab Legion in March 1956. At the same time, French hatred of the Egyptian leader intensified as the war in Algeria developed and his support for the FLN seemed to grow stronger; in the United States, Dulles began to regard Nasser as a communist sympathiser because of the arms deal with Czechoslovakia. By mid-1956 Egypt was becoming progressively isolated from the West.

The results were inevitable. On 19 July 1956 the Egyptians were informed that both Britain and the United States had reconsidered the offer of their loan, despite assurances of assistance made earlier the same day, and this obviously affected the attitude of the World Bank. There were a number of reasons for this sudden *volte face* by the Western powers, not least a genuine feeling that the Egyptian economy could not bear a

debt of 1400 million dollars, but this did nothing to lessen the insult felt by Nasser. At a public meeting in Cairo two days later he announced that the Egyptian government would finance the project from its own resources. On 26 July his method of achieving this was reported to Sir Anthony Eden while he was at dinner in London. Egypt had nationalised the Anglo-French Suez Canal Company – compensating the shareholders – and foreign currency revenues from the Canal tolls would be used to build the High Dam.

A cynical collusion

The Anglo-French reaction, despite various nods in the direction of diplomacy, was principally a military one, designed to rid the Middle East of Nasser's influence once and for all. Both countries mobilised their military resources, an expeditionary force was prepared and a plan – codenamed Operation Musketeer – was formulated to invade Egypt as a 'police action'. But United States pressure for a peaceful solution, combined with Egyptian assurances that the Canal would stay fully operational as an international waterway in accordance with the Treaty of Constantinople of 1888, made the use of force difficult to justify. What was needed was an excuse.

This was provided by the Israelis, through their contacts with the French,

and although the thought of collusion with the Jews was repugnant to many traditionally pro-Arab Britons, the potential advantages of concerted military action were attractive. By 13 October 1956 Eden was aware of Israeli plans for an attack into Sinai, designed to destroy the Egyptian and Palestinian menace in a military campaign, and on 25 October he met with Guy Mollet of France and David Ben-Gurion of Israel at Sèvres, just outside Paris, to sign an agreement for cooperation in the overthrow of Nasser. Operation Musketeer was consequently revised, providing for an Anglo-French invasion of Port Said, at the northern end of the Suez Canal, some time after the Israeli invasion of Sinai. The pretext would be to separate the belligerents (Egypt and Israel) for the safety of the Canal and its users and in the name of the United Nations. The attack was to be preceded by an ultimatum requiring both sides to pull back 16km (10 miles) from the Canal, something that would clearly be rejected by the Egyptians as impracticable and an insult to their territorial integrity. It seemed a neat, if extremely cynical plan. France made no attempt to disguise her support for Israel in the weeks before the war: three French warships appeared off the Israeli coast, a squadron of Mystère IVs was flown by French pilots from Israeli airfields and supplies of military equipment were increased. The scene was set for the second round of the Arab-Israeli conflict.

4. The Sinai Campaign of 1956

At 1600 hours on Monday, 29 October 1956, the lead elements of the Israeli 202nd Parachute Brigade, commanded by Colonel Ariel ('Arik') Sharon, crossed into Egyptian territory at Suweilma. Fifty-nine minutes later, 395 paratroops from the same brigade, led by Lieutenant-Colonel Rafael ('Raful') Eitan, dropped from 16 C–47 transport aircraft near the Mitla Pass in western Sinai. Because of faulty navigation, they actually landed some 5km (3 miles) to the east of their intended dropping zone – a limestone obelisk known as Parker's Memorial, situated about 25km (15 miles) east of the Pass. Thirteen paras were slightly injured in the drop and it took the unit

two-and-a-half hours to regroup and reach the obelisk, where they dug in. The rest of the brigade was to make a dash across Sinai and link up with them within 48 hours.

This was the opening move of the Israelis' Operation Kadesh, the overall aims of which were to destroy the Palestinian menace in the Gaza Strip, ensure free maritime movement through the Gulf of Aqaba by the occupation of Sharm el Sheikh at the southern tip of Sinai overlooking the Straits of Tiran, and to impose a crushing military defeat, in conjunction with the French and British expeditionary force, upon the Egyptians. The pretext for action was

provided by the death of three Israeli soldiers on 21 October in the Al Auja demilitarised zone, when their vehicles hit Egyptian land mines, but as collusion with the European states was by then well advanced, this was little more than a convenient excuse. To all three of the attacking powers, the main aim was the humiliation and overthrow of Nasser.

The probability of the Anglo-French intervention was of great strategic value to the Israelis, enabling them to take risks which would have been otherwise unjustified. Fearing a British and French invasion of the Nile Delta, Nasser had thinned out his forces in Sinai and redeployed them around Alexandria as

early as August 1956. Thus when the Israelis attacked, Egypt's striking force of armoured units was located west of the Canal and, as there was only one bridge capable of taking such heavy traffic across the Canal (at Firdan, to the south of El Qantara) reinforcement to the east was unlikely to be swift.

Axes of advance

The Israeli invasion forces attacked on four axes of advance, following the four roads across the peninsula. The units were grouped into task forces, one for each of the axes. The northern axis was assigned to Group 77, consisting of the 1st and 11th Infantry Brigades and the 27th Armoured Brigade, and followed the line Gaza Strip – El Arish – El Qantara. The central axis (Al Auja – El Quseima – Abu Aweigila – Bir Gifgafa – Ismailiya) was assigned to Group 38, composed of the 7th and 37th Armoured Brigades and the 4th and 10th Infantry Brigades. It was on this axis that the fiercest fighting took place, as had been anticipated. The southern axis (El Kuntilla – El Thamad – Nakhl – Mitla Pass) was the task of Sharon's 202nd Paratroop Brigade. It was to be joined by a battalion of the 12th Infantry Brigade for a dash down

the western axis to Sharm el Sheikh. The eastern axis (down the Gulf of Aqaba to Sharm el Sheikh) was the task of the 9th Infantry Brigade. The deception plan was to disguise the invasion as a raid.

Because of this, the only major penetration during the first 48 hours was to be along the undefended southern axis to the Mitla Pass, and no armoured units were to be engaged during this time. Quseima (central axis) and Ras el Naqb (eastern axis) were to be taken by infantry units and held. This was initially to protect the flanks of the southern axis, and later to provide jumping-off points for attacks along the central and western axes. These attacks were scheduled to take place after the British and French air forces had neutralised Egyptian air power. It was only to be on the night of 31 October that the give-away invasion sign of armoured advances was to take place on the central and northern axes. The 9th Infantry Brigade was to start its advance on Sharm el Sheikh on 1 November.

Advancing against orders

General Moshe Dayan, the Israeli chief of staff, ordered Group 38 to halt after the infantry assault on Quseima. The 7th Armoured Brigade was to be kept 'silent,

motionless, unobtrusive' for 48 hours at Nahal Ruth in dead ground behind Al Auja. But the IDF is often beset by the insubordination and disobedience to orders of its commanders. The group commander, Major-General Assaf Simhoni, ordered the 7th Armoured Brigade

Forces engaged in Sinai

	tanks	guns	aircraft	men
Egypt	150	140	60	40,000
Israel	180	150	130	45,000

Opposite: Israeli troops take cover during the fighting in the Gaza Strip against determined Egyptian defence. Above right: Moshe Dayan, chief of staff of the Israeli Army from 1953 to 1958, was largely responsible for the success of Operation Kadesh. Right: Israeli soldiers on the heights above El Quseima, shortly before they took the town on 30 October 1956.

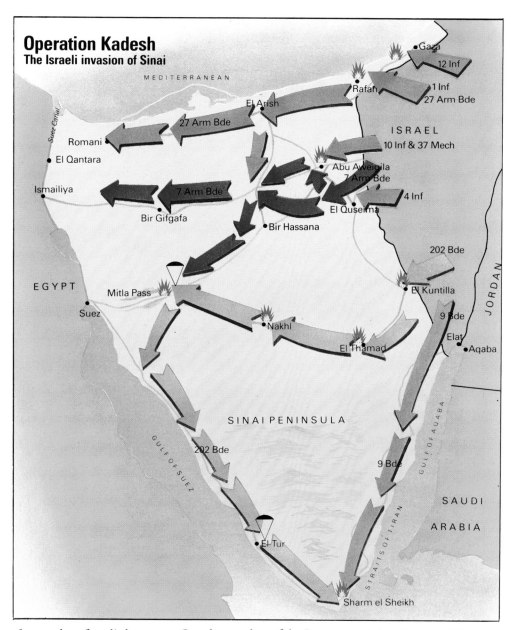

Operation Kadesh
The Israeli invasion of Sinai

forward at first light on 30 October and sent it beyond Quseima and northwards to Abu Aweigila, where it encountered Egyptian positions and was brought to a bloody halt in the full light of day. The gaff was blown. Dayan was furious, but did the only thing he could have done in the circumstances – he ordered the advance on the central axis to be speeded up.

On the afternoon of the previous day, Sharon's paratroopers had jumped on the Parker's Memorial dropping zone. The original DZ had been at the western end of the Mitla Pass, but aerial photographs had shown tents and vehicles there. These belonged to a construction camp and not to soldiers, but the Israelis did not know that and so the DZ was changed less than 24 hours before H-hour to the eastern end

of the Pass, some 64km (40 miles) from the Canal. It was not thought to matter that much, for it could still be announced that the Israelis were at the Mitla Pass and thus threatening the Canal: this was vital for the collusion plan with the British and French. During the night of 29/30 October the Israelis in fact stated that their forces had reached a point only 29km (18 miles) east of Suez.

During the night, six French-piloted Nord Atlas transports air-dropped heavy weapons, ammunition, water, food and medical supplies to the battalion at Parker's Memorial. These had been arranged in advance with General André Beaufre, the deputy land force commander in the Anglo-French expeditionary force. The planes flew back and forth for

two days between Cyprus and the Israeli airbase at Ekron outside Tel Aviv. From there they flew to Mitla. The heavy equipment included eight jeeps, four 106mm recoilless anti-tank rifles, and two 120mm medium mortars.

Egyptian reinforcements

At 2000 hours on the night of 29/30 October the Egyptian Eastern Command ordered two infantry battalions, the 5th and 6th at Fayid, to prepare to move against the Israelis at Mitla. At 2100, the 5th Infantry Battalion began crossing the Canal by means of a chain-ferry north of Suez. It was under strict orders not to interfere with the passage of shipping down the Canal: the Egyptians were anxious not to give the British and French any excuse to intervene to protect commercial users' interests. The battalion got across in eight hours. At daylight, the amount of shipping increased and it took the 6th Infantry Battalion 12 hours to cross. Kuntilla fell to the Israelis at 2100 hours on 29 October.

By 2300 on 29 October, President Nasser and his generals had finished their appreciation of the situation. The two full-strength brigades of the 4th Armoured Division were ordered across the Canal. Each brigade had 55 Soviet T–34 tanks and 20 Su–100 self-propelled guns. Their task was to assemble at Bir Gifgafa and Bir Rod Salem on the Israelis' central axis, and from there to send detachments south through Wadi Mleiz to cut off the paratroops at the Mitla Pass and block any further Israeli moves on the central and northern axes. The same restrictions about not impeding civilian shipping using the Canal were applied to them as to the infantry. As a result, the first brigade did not reach Bir Gifgafa until 1500 hours on 30 October and the second brigade did not complete its Canal crossing until first light on the 31st.

On the morning of 30 October the Anglo-French ultimatum, demanding an end to the fighting and a withdrawal of all units – Egyptian as well as Israeli – away from the Canal, under threat of military intervention by the European states, was delivered to Cairo and Tel Aviv. When presenting it to the House of Commons, Sir Anthony Eden claimed that 'the Israeli spearhead was not far from the banks' of the Canal. However, at that time the only serious fighting was some 200km (124 miles) away from the Canal at Abu Aweigila. The only Israelis anywhere near the waterway were the paras at the Mitla Pass, who were digging in. As the morning mists disappeared in the heat, the Israelis found that Parker's Memorial was in fact held by an Egyptian platoon, and four companies of the 5th Infantry Battalion were astride the entrance to the Pass on Jebel Heitan and Jebel Giddi. At 0830 the platoon at the Memorial opened fire on the Israelis below them. The Israelis tried three times during the morning to dislodge the Egyptians but failed each time. The

Opposite: The Israeli advance into Sinai was a demonstration of the power of mobile warfare. Right: Colonel Ariel 'Arik' Sharon, whose forces' actions in the Mitla Pass were later severely criticised for the casualties they caused. Below: Israeli infantry advance up a hillside in Sinai.

battalion commander decided to wait it out in his defensive positions until the rest of the brigade arrived at nightfall.

Sharon at the Mitla Pass

The rest of Sharon's brigade pushed towards the Mitla Pass with as much speed as they could muster. Reports were received from aerial reconnaissance of the Egyptian armour concentrating at Bir Gifgafa, and Sharon felt that this threat to his brigade was sufficient to force him to seize a more defensible position. He determined to move deeper into the Pass as soon as he arrived, even though his orders were to stay outside the eastern end. His brigade suffered its first battle casualties during an attack on

Themed, just after first light on 30 October. The frontier post there was defended by a company of Sudanese infantry armed with bolt-action Lee Enfield rifles, some heavy machine-guns and some recoilless rifles. The post was the only prepared defensive position on the southern axis. Although it was protected by mines and wire, these were really designed to keep out smugglers and not to obstruct a combined armour and infantry attack.

The Sudanese troops' standing orders were to withdraw in the face of superior Israeli forces. They ignored these, and engaged in a 40-minute battle with the Israelis, killing four and wounding six. The defenders suffered an estimated 50 killed before they withdrew in jeeps to Nakhl some 65km (40 miles) to the north-west, where they joined the Egyptian infantry company garrisoning the area. During the battle for Thamad the Egyptian Air Force flew its first fighter ground attack mission of the war. In an early morning strafing attack, four British-made Vampire and four Soviet-built MiG-15 jet aircraft fired on the Israelis, hitting three of their soldiers.
(*Continued on page 42.*)

The Assault on Suez

The plans for the Anglo-French invasion of Suez were eventually to involve 90,000 military personnel, 500 aircraft and 130 warships. The operation was to involve two main phases; an airborne assault of approximately battalion strength, to be followed by a waterborne assault carrying the main force.

Shortly after dawn on 5 November 1956, 600 British paratroopers from the 3rd Battalion the Parachute Regiment and 487 French paratroopers from the 2nd Regiment FCPD (French Colonial Parachute Division), were dropped into their respective landing zones. The British drop zone was Gamil, Port Said's airstrip, some 1600m (1 mile) long and 800m ($\frac{1}{2}$ mile) wide. The main problem facing this relatively inexperienced parachute force was the narrowness of the drop zone which, being coastal, was also usually subject to strong ground winds. In order to overcome the possibility of high casualties through drift, the British decided to make the drop at 180m (600ft). The time allowed for the drop was eight minutes. The British force was to hit their drop zone some 15 minutes before the French.

The British drop was certainly hindered by both unsuitable equipment and lack of experience. Indeed it was fortunate that Egyptian resistance on the ground was not deployed in force as the British made their jumps completely separately from their equipment. This meant that they had no form of protection against ground fire and that they had to locate equipment canisters before they could actually move against the enemy. Some protection, however, was afforded to the assault force by sand-filled oil drums which the Egyptians had used to block the runway against a possible landing. Within 30 minutes the airstrip was secured. This initial success was intended to be followed up by a rapid occupation of Port Said itself, but stiff resistance along the approaches to the town forced the British troops to take up defensive positions around the perimeter and to await the arrival of the seaborne group the following day.

The French dropping zone was at Raswa, with a view to securing vital bridges in the area. The zone itself was a strip of land some 800m ($\frac{1}{2}$ mile) long and 140m (150yd) wide. The French made their drop from a height of 120m (400ft) within a four-minute time frame and, at a cost of only ten casualties, secured their objectives. Within the hour they had taken the only remaining bridge over the Interior Basin. The success of the French drop contrasted strongly with that of the British, probably because many of the French paras were veterans of drops in Indochina and Algeria. Indeed, having managed to send patrols up to 10km (6 miles) south and having encountered no Egyptian resistance, the French launched a further drop during the afternoon in order to secure Port Fuad. The vanguard now awaited the arrival of the seaborne forces.

At 0450 hours on 6 November 1956, after an hour-long naval bombardment, 40 and 42 Commando, Royal Marines, hit the beaches either side of the Casino pier on the Port Said seafront. While 40 and 42 Commando, with Centurions from 'C' sqn 6th Royal Tank Regiment

Opposite above: The airborne operation was an essential part of the Anglo-French plans to take Port Said. Above: Paratroopers wait to drop. Above right and right: British paras form up and prepare to go into action after the drop on the airfield.

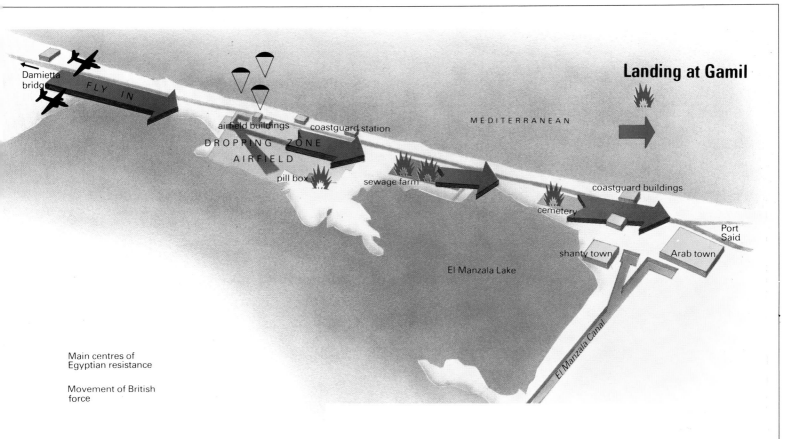

Landing at Gamil

Damietta bridge

FLY IN

airfield buildings

coastguard station

MEDITERRANEAN

DROPPING ZONE
AIRFIELD

pill box

sewage farm

coastguard buildings

cemetery

Port Said

shanty town

Arab town

El Manzala Lake

El Manzala Canal

Main centres of
Egyptian resistance

Movement of British
force

in support, pushed quickly through Port Said in order to establish a link-up with French forces at the Raswa bridge, 45 Commando, who had been brought from the fleet (HMS *Ocean* and HMS *Theseus*) by helicopter, directed much of their offensive toward clearing snipers from the streets and destroying enemy positions which the vanguard had bypassed. They were helped in this by the renewed offensive of 3rd Parachute Brigade from the west.

The French offensive against Port Fuad, which went in at 0645 hours, deployed one parachute regiment, three marine commando units and a squadron of AMX battle tanks. Once again the French operation contrasted strongly with the British, and with ruthless determination all resistance to the French in Port Fuad was completely crushed. The Egyptian defenders in Port Said, on the other hand, continued to fight through the afternoon. Late in the afternoon of 6 November, however, the British 16th Parachute Brigade was moved into Port Said in order to take the harbour areas which could then facilitate naval clearing operations. The area was taken without

casualties. At the same time, British Centurion tanks were advancing southward, reaching El Tina by nightfall, in an attempt to expand the amount of territory under Anglo-French control. With the announcement, at 1900 hours, of a cease-fire effective from midnight, French para-troopers commandeered any vehicles they could find in order to use the remaining time to establish firmly the Allied beach-head. At midnight on 6 November hostilities ceased.

The forces at Suez			
Phase one Air bombardment 31 Oct–4 Nov 1956	Valiants, Canberras, Venoms, Hunters and Thunderstreaks operating out of Malta and Cyprus Combined naval task force of Sea Hawks, Sea Venoms, Corsairs and Thunderstreaks operating from carriers 50 miles off the coast of Egypt		
	British forces		**French forces**
Phase two Airborne assault 5 Nov 1956	**main force** 3rd Parachute Battalion Group – Gamil airfield		parachute battalion group of 10th Parachute Div – Raswa and Port Fouad
	reserve force 1st Battalion Royal West Kent Regt		two parachute regts 10th Parachute Div
Phase three Seaborne assault morning 6 Nov 1956	3rd Commando Brigade Royal Marines comprising 40 Commando, 42 Commando, 45 Commando C Sqn 6th Royal Tank Regt 3rd Field Sqn Royal Engineers		parachute battalion of 10th Parachute Div 3 Marine Commandos one sqn AMX tanks
Immediate seaborne follow-up 6–7 Nov 1956	two battalions 16th Parachute Bde and supporting arms 6th Royal Tank Regt		one sqn AMX tanks one sqn Patton tanks one engineer company

Sharon's drive through Sinai
29 – 31 Oct 1956

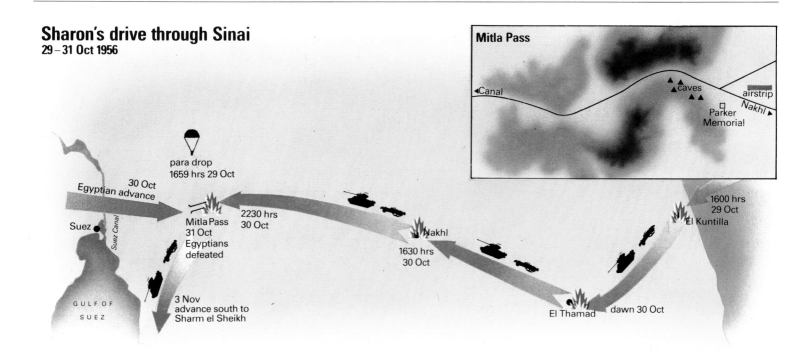

Rearguard actions

The Sudanese joined the Egyptians around the anti-smuggling post at Nakhl, a place with no prepared defences and no normal strategic function. The two companies, knowing that their withdrawal route through the Mitla Pass was cut, prepared to fight a delaying action so that they could escape while the Israelis regrouped and deployed again. Just before sunset, Sharon's brigade arrived. With three battalions of infantry and supporting armour and artillery he attacked the open post, the defending infantry of which had no anti-armour weapons left. After a brief and bloody firefight, during which they suffered 56 killed and a number of wounded, the defenders successfully managed to withdraw, escaping into the wadis of the surrounding desert.

Needing to conserve their aircraft for close air support in a major battle against Abu Aweigila on 31 October, Sharon was ordered to refrain from any further battles that day. However, overestimating the threat from Egyptian armour at Bir Gifgafa, he was anxious to gain a more defensible position. So, having secured permission for a small patrol to enter the Pass, he determined to seize the ground by sending a battalion-sized combined-arms force in. He underestimated the numbers of Egyptians there, thinking that their 5th and 6th Infantry Battalions had been practically destroyed by Israeli air strikes. In fact, the 5th Battalion (plus one company of the 6th) was well-positioned on both sides of the Heitan Defile, in some caves on the Jebel Heitan lying on the south side of the Pass, and in dug-outs along the ridges to the north. They were also well-equipped with heavy weapons.

At 1230 on 31 October, the Israelis entered the defile and immediately came under fire from both flanks, the leading two half-tracks being hit. The troops deployed and took cover behind boulders, where they were pinned down by Egyp-

tian fire. The force commander drove on in his half-track until it went off the trail into a wadi while trying to shunt the wreck of an Egyptian truck out of the way. The rest of the force drove on into the saucer between the Mitla and Heitan Defiles, where they were strafed by Egyptian MiG–15s. The brigade reconnaissance unit tried to clear the ridges, but came under fire from the caves and had to withdraw with heavy casualties. By mounting a combined attack from the saucer and from the east, the Israelis were eventually able to capture the ridges by nightfall. After dark, they sent fighting patrols to take out the caves. For two-and-a-half hours, the battle raged in the dark. Under cover of the confusion caused by the firefight, the Egyptians began to withdraw in response to orders from Cairo. These had been prompted by the first British air raids by Canberra and Valiant bombers on Gameel airbase ordered when the ultimatum of the previous day had failed to produce any positive response. The Israelis also withdrew from the Pass to Parker's Memorial, where they laid up and regrouped for nearly two days. Sharon's brigade lost 38 killed and 120 wounded in the fighting. The Egyptians lost over 200 killed. Dayan's comment was that 'this battle was not essential'.

The Egyptian plan now was to disengage in Sinai, and so keep the bulk of

Opposite above: Sharon's Sinai Campaign.
Opposite below: The debris of the
Egyptian retreat. Above: The Israeli flag in
Sharm el Sheikh. Above right and right:
Israeli troops prepare for attack. Below:
Half-tracks roar off into the desert.

the army intact for the anticipated battle against the British and French. To this end, many of their battles in the peninsula were to help the withdrawal and to buy time. It was to cover the withdrawal from Gaza and El Arish, and to prevent the Israelis attacking the retreating troops from the flank, that the Egyptian resistance at Abu Aweigila was aimed. The deployment of the two armoured brigades at Bir Gifgafa and Bir Rod Salem was intended to support this battle by

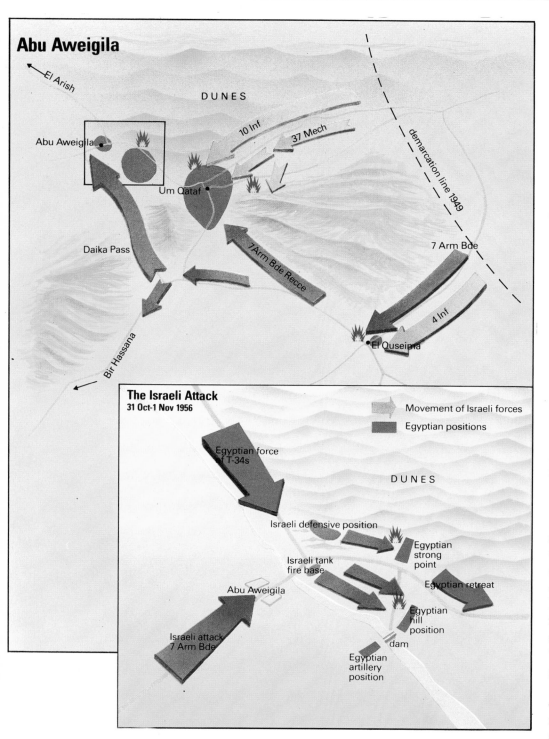

Abu Aweigila

El Arish

DUNES

Abu Aweigila

10 Inf

37 Mech

demarcation line 1949

Um Qataf

Daika Pass

7 Arm Bde Recce

7 Arm Bde

4 Inf

El Quseima

Bir Hassana

The Israeli Attack
31 Oct-1 Nov 1956

Movement of Israeli forces

Egyptian positions

Egyptian force of T-34s

DUNES

Israeli defensive position

Israeli tank fire base

Egyptian strong point

Egyptian retreat

Abu Aweigila

Egyptian hill position

dam

Israeli attack 7 Arm Bde

Egyptian artillery position

Left: The assault at Abu Aweigila that was the major action of the Sinai Campaign, with attackers and defenders giving all they had. Opposite: The Israeli withdrawal from Sinai in December 1956, following the UN intervention. Destroyed Egyptian transport litters the landscape. Opposite right: Israeli armoured cars in the Gaza Strip. The Gaza Strip, a thin finger of coastal land going into Israel, was an irritating strategic problem for the Israeli forces.

the village, and was held by the 6th Infantry Brigade under Brigadier-General Sami Yassa. The three-day-long battle for the position was the principal action of the Sinai War between the Egyptians and the Israelis. It was of epic proportions, with the Egyptians fighting stubbornly and bravely and, in the end, without air support, rations or water. Yassa had at his disposal the 17th and 18th Infantry Battalions, the 3rd Field Artillery Regiment, the 78th and 94th Antitank Batteries, two companies of reservists, and a light reconnaissance company mounted in jeeps. In the divisional reserve at El Arish was the 4th Infantry Brigade under Colonel Saadeddin Mutawally, which was only two battalions strong (the 10th and 12th Infantry). During the battle, Colonel Mutawally took over command of the Abu Aweigila defence after Brigadier Yassa was wounded while personally leading a counter-attack. The 12th Infantry Battalion, plus some supporting arms, was also sent to the position. Thus a beefed-up Egyptian infantry brigade faced four Israeli brigades (4th and 10th Infantry, and 7th and 37th Armoured) that were supported by the most modern fighter planes in the Middle East at the time – the Dassault Mystère IV. It was during this battle that French-piloted Mystères attacked the Egyptian positions and vehicles with rockets and napalm.

The defenders of Abu Aweigila fulfilled their mission, and successfully fought off Israeli attacks against their shrinking perimeter with heavy losses on both sides in men and equipment. The Israelis eventually entered the position at midday on 2 November, nearly 24 hours after the defenders had slipped through their

acting as a counter-penetration force.

The Egyptian government had originally, on the night of 29 October, believed that Britain and France did not intend to intervene physically, but the ultimatum, followed by the British air attacks, convinced them otherwise. All units that had been ordered into Sinai to fight the Israeli invasion were ordered to withdraw west of the Canal to meet the greater threat. Forces in place had to fight first a covering action and then a withdrawal

from contact – the most difficult of all military tasks. Abu Aweigila was ordered to be held until the night of 1 November, when its defenders would withdraw under cover of darkness, leaving small rearguards to delay the Israeli follow-up.

Abu Aweigila

The Abu Aweigila position was actually based on a strategic hill, called Um Qataf, some 15km (9 miles) to the east of

lines and withdrawn to the west. The ferocity of the defence had therefore bought the Egyptians a day more than ordered.

Israel's allies

Anglo-French help to the Israeli campaign was not limited to the neutralising of the Egyptian Air Force and the bombing of military bases and convoys. French pilots flew Mystère IVs in action against Egyptian aircraft and against ground targets. The Israelis managed to capture the Egyptian destroyer *Ibrahim el Awal* after it had bombarded Haifa naval base. Its escape was intercepted by a French destroyer flotilla and it engaged in a gun-battle with the *Kersaint* – one of the French warships. The delay allowed it to be caught by the Israelis. At 0100 on the morning of 1 November, the Egyptian destroyer *Damietta* was sunk by the Royal Navy cruiser HMS *Newfoundland* in the Red Sea. The ship had been sailing to the assistance of the garrison at Sharm el Sheikh when it met the unlit *Newfoundland* and its escorting destroyers. A brisk gun-exchange followed, and the *Damietta* was sunk while trying to ram the British cruiser. During the battle for Rafah in the Gaza Strip, the French Navy provided naval gunfire support to the attacking Israeli troops and shelled Egyptian positions during the early morning of 1 November from the cruiser *Georges Leygues* and destroyers.

The Egyptian commander at Rafah, Brigadier-General Jaafer al-Abd, conducted a brilliant withdrawal from contact. Ordered to retreat by Cairo while his forces were engaged in a fierce battle with the Israelis, and under a naval bombardment from the French, he managed to extricate the bulk of his brigade intact and withdraw west of the Canal even after the loss of El Arish which lay on his route out.

Sharm el Sheikh falls

The final action of the Israeli campaign in Sinai was the capture of Sharm el Sheikh on 5 November. The Israelis had been inflicting heavy casualties on the defenders by air attacks using bombs, rockets and napalm for three days, starting at 0900 on 2 November. When the Egyptian commander, Colonel Raouf Mahfouz Zaki, learned from the interrogation of a captured pilot of a downed Mystère that the Israelis were advancing in a two-pronged attack against his position, he ordered the perimeter to be shrunk onto Sharm el Sheikh. The defenders were withdrawn from Ras Nasrani (to the north-east) and redeployed in the main location. When the Israeli 9th Brigade put in its attack against the position on 4 November it was already two days behind schedule and the government was beginning to worry that it might not be able to spin the war out much longer against mounting international pressure. As one of the principal objectives of the campaign was the capture of Sharm el Sheikh and the securing of Israeli passage through the Straits of Tiran which it dominated, a failure to take the position before hostilities were brought to an end would mean that the war had been largely fruitless.

Israeli aircraft attacked the position all day on 4 November and just after midnight the 9th Brigade put in its first attack supported by tanks. The Egyptians beat them off and the Israelis withdrew at 0430 on 5 November. An hour later, at 0530, the 9th Brigade put in a daylight attack. This time they were supported by air strikes, tanks, airborne forward air controllers and artillery and mortar observers. Waves of aircraft dived on the position with bombs, rockets and napalm, and the Israeli tanks drove onto the defences behind this storm. The emplacements had to be captured one by one in an hour of fierce fighting, but by 0900 the battle was over. The Israelis had lost 10 killed and 32 wounded, but the Egyptian defenders had over 100 killed and 31 wounded. The Sinai Campaign was over.

The United Nations Emergency Force

The Israelis had achieved their objectives only just in time, for on 6 November, with international pressure – particularly from the United States and Soviet Union – mounting, a ceasefire was imposed. In its aftermath, the Israelis tried to negotiate a permanent settlement of the two main issues that had led to war – freedom of passage through the Straits of Tiran and control of the *fedayeen* in the Gaza Strip – but with little success. In the end a United Nations Emergency Force was created to stand between the Egyptians and Israelis on the borders of Sinai after the latter had withdrawn back to the positions they had occupied before the war began. An uneasy peace ensued that was to last for over ten years, but as the basic problems of Israel – her weak strategic and economic positions in the Middle East – had not been solved, it could never be regarded as permanent. The only consolation for Israel was that the IDF had gained invaluable experience, particularly in the deserts and mountains of Sinai. It was to prove useful in 1967.

5. Nationalism and Revolution, 1956-'67

Although Egyptian forces were severely mauled in the Suez Campaign of 1956, Nasser emerged triumphant. The Anglo-French intervention on the side of Israel had transformed Nasser's personal position from one of being yet another military ruler into a national leader – although at times this was to work against him, for he was held in such high esteem that he frequently became a prisoner of his own reputation. Suez had shown that the Arabs were no longer impotent and that even the mighty British could be humbled and humiliated. Iraq and Jordan were unable to resist joining the other Arab states in their condemnation of Britain and France.

Nasser's reputation after Suez was so high that some Arabs sought to join with him in creating a new Pan-Arab world; others turned to him to solve their own problems. This was the case with Syria,

The young King Hussein of Jordan (left) is greeted by Nasser (right) in Cairo in 1957 during a conference with other Arab Heads of State.

which now sought a union with Egypt. But Syria was divided, the Sunn'ite Moslems in the south favouring union with Iraq while the communists looked to Moscow for an alliance, for the Russians were now seeking to woo the Arab world. The Americans, anxious to recover ground, countered with the Eisenhower Doctrine – a promise of aid and assistance to any Arab state that was prepared to show sympathy with the West. Jordan, Iraq and Saudi Arabia, all of whom feared the radicalism of Nasser, showed some interest.

The United Arab Republic

In the end it was the recently-formed Ba'athist Party which led the initiative for a union between Syria and Egypt. Ba'athism, which means 'resurrection' or 'renaissance', was a political movement first formed in 1952, embracing the ideology of Pan-Arab nationalism together with some concepts of a French style of socialism. The Ba'athist appeal was something which Nasser found irresistible. Union with Syria would give Egypt an influence in the very heart of the Fertile Crescent, from where it could launch its offensive against the Hashemites and Saudi Arabia. It would help to resolve the dilemma of Egypt, a state which was much larger than other Arab states in terms of population, yet isolated geographically and devoid of natural resources. Without material wealth, Egypt could not sustain any drive for leadership in the Arab world.

On 1 February 1958 Syria and Egypt joined together in the United Arab

Republic (UAR). The new capital was Cairo and Nasser the first Head of State. Though the constitution allowed for two Syrian and two Egyptian vice-presidents, Field-Marshal Abdul Hakin Amer, a close personal friend and confidant, functioned as Nasser's 'viceroy' in Damascus. The spectre of a union between two radical and hostile powers galvanised Jordan and Iraq into action. The Hashemite cousins responded with their own union the same month, which they called the Arab Federation. Feisal of Iraq became Head of State and Hussein of Jordan his deputy. The Federation raised the banner flown by their great-grandfather Sharif Hussain during the Arab Revolt against the Turk.

On paper at least the union of these two countries presented a formidable alliance. Geographically contiguous, Iraq was oil rich and could use its wealth to fuel the economy of a resource-starved but militarily impressive Jordan. However, the Arab Federation was short-lived and destined to end in tragedy. It was the outbreak of civil war in Lebanon in 1958 and the death of Feisal, his family and court in a bloody revolution in Iraq in the same year, that spelt its doom.

In Lebanon the delicate balance between Christian and Moslem enshrined in the French-designed constitution came apart at the seams. The Arabs demanded that Lebanon should join with the UAR and their hero Nasser; thousands flocked to Damascus to see him. The Christian president, Camille Chamoun, coldly ambitious, was not only resolutely set against such a move but was also about to set aside the constitution to seek a second

Above: Feisal of Iraq, the young monarch who was to die in 1958, with his Prince Regent in 1952.

Below: The British 16th Independent Parachute Brigade in Jordan in 1958. King Hussein had asked for British help after the coup in Iraq had threatened the stability of his own country. But British influence in the Middle East was steadily declining during the 1950s and 1960s (right), adding to the instability of the region.

six-year term of office. There was considerable turmoil and civil disorder.

Slaughter in Baghdad

In Iraq the old prime minister, Nuri Said, now made a fatal blunder. He ordered Iraqi divisions under the command of General Kassim to march into Jordan, the intention probably being to invade Syria. Instead Kassim and his subordinates, led by Colonel Abdul Salam Aref, marched their troops on the Iraqi capital, Baghdad. On 14 July 1958, the king, royal family and court were slaughtered. Kassim proclaimed a republic with himself as president. A single bloody blow had destroyed the main bastion of support for the West in the Fertile Crescent and the Arab world.

Meanwhile, violence in Beirut flared into civil war and the Lebanese government appealed to the United States for assistance under the terms of the Eisenhower Doctrine. The United States Sixth Fleet, undisputed master of the eastern Mediterranean, sent its Marine Task Force ashore and rapidly restored order. At the same time King Hussein of Jordan, desperate to contain the repercussions of the ill-fated Arab Federation, welcomed

British paratroopers into Amman. The Anglo-American operations were textbook examples of successful military intervention in support of client regimes. Nasser's progress was halted and the Iraqi revolution contained.

Contrary to many expectations at the time, revolutionary Iraq did not join the UAR. Kassim was a nationalist first and an Arabist second. He proceeded to rule the country with the support of a small but vociferous Communist Party, and this in turn aroused the hostility of Egypt. Colonel Aref, being a member of the Iraqi Ba'athist Party, contested the decision of his leader and was condemned to death for treason. Kassim commuted the sentence against his young subordinate in an act of clemency which he was later to regret.

South Arabia

Events in southern Arabia now caused the Arabs to concentrate on this hitherto rather quiet part of the Middle East. It was an area where the British were still entrenched militarily, though they had been attempting to create a viable political structure to counter the threat from radical Arabs. Britain planned a Federation based on the tribal Sheikhs of the

Waning British power in the Middle East

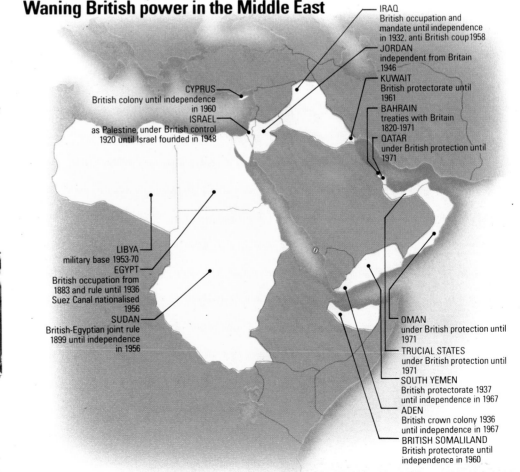

CYPRUS
British colony until independence in 1960

ISRAEL
as Palestine, under British control 1920 until Israel founded in 1948

LIBYA
military base 1953-70

EGYPT
British occupation from 1883 and rule until 1936 Suez Canal nationalised 1956

SUDAN
British-Egyptian joint rule 1899 until independence in 1956

IRAQ
British occupation and mandate until independence in 1932, anti British coup 1958

JORDAN
independent from Britain 1946

KUWAIT
British protectorate until 1961

BAHRAIN
treaties with Britain 1820-1971

QATAR
under British protection until 1971

OMAN
under British protection until 1971

TRUCIAL STATES
under British protection until 1971

SOUTH YEMEN
British protectorate 1937 until independence in 1967

ADEN
British crown colony 1936 until independence in 1967

BRITISH SOMALILAND
British protectorate until independence in 1960

interior and the Sultan of the Aden Protectorate. This was vehemently opposed by the reactionary Imam Ahmed in the neighbouring country of Yemen. He 'associated' his realm with the UAR, partly to protect his interests in the region and partly as insurance against the wrath of the radicals.

With Egyptian support, Yemen sponsored sabotage and terrorism among the disaffected and unruly tribes of the interior. Despite this campaign of intimidation, six of the Sheikhs accepted the proposed Federation in 1959. London then attempted to find some means of associating the Federation with Aden, though it had no intention of abandoning the excellent harbour and base facilities.

Nasser's involvement in the Yemen

The 1960s were to prove a turbulent time for Nasser. Despite the fanfares, there had been problems from the outset with the Syrians. The Ba'athists had soon become disenchanted with Nasser's preferred style of military rule and moved into opposition. Neither did Egypt have the resources

Aden

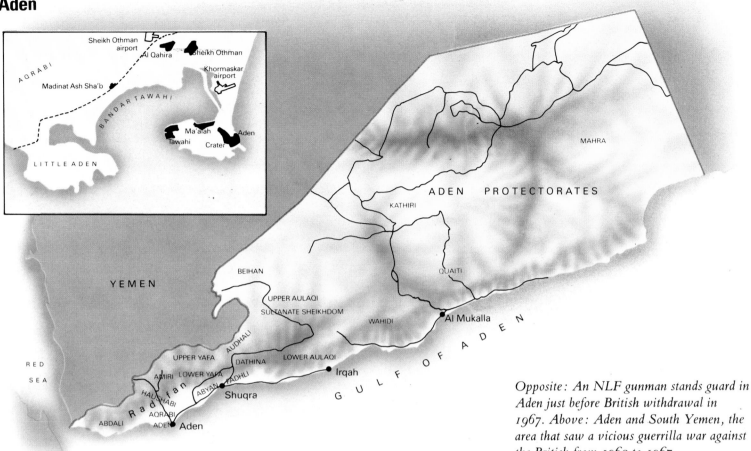

Opposite: An NLF gunman stands guard in Aden just before British withdrawal in 1967. Above: Aden and South Yemen, the area that saw a vicious guerrilla war against the British from 1963 to 1967.

to bridge the geographical gap between the two countries, and the UAR experiment moved inevitably towards failure. In September 1961 a Syrian coup brought a nationalist group of officers to power and the union ended.

The fragility of Arab unity was also demonstrated elsewhere in 1961. Britain withdrew from Kuwait and this was the signal for Kassim to claim the country for Iraq. Nasser could not allow a powerful, oil-rich, Soviet-backed Iraq to emerge in the Gulf any more than could the conservative-minded Saudi Arabians. Both gave their tacit support to the redeployment of British troops to counter the Iraqi threat and later helped replace them with forces from the Arab League.

In September 1961 the Imam Ahmed of the Yemen died and was succeeded by his son Muhammad al Badr. A group of republican army officers, led by Brigadier Sallal, rebelled and seized the main towns. Badr escaped into the country and rallied support among the hill tribes. The Yemeni republicans successfully appealed to Nasser for military aid and assistance.

What little unity that remained in the Arab world at this time was further fragmented by Saudi Arabia supporting Badr and the royalist faction. The military presence of a radical Egypt in southern Arabia was viewed with the deepest misgivings by the Saudis.

In the years that followed, the Egyptian Expeditionary Force in Yemen was built up to a strength of 50,000 men in a war which later became known as 'Nasser's Vietnam'. The Egyptians, ill-trained for a counter-insurgency war in a strange and mountainous terrain, could make little progress against the royalist tribes. Pacification policies simply resulted in the wholesale destruction of villages and the alienation of the local population. The war was further complicated by the attitudes of the Federation and Aden. The Sheikhs supported the royalist cause, which in turn exposed them to guerrilla counterattacks. The urbanised Adenis favoured the republicans, hated the thought of a merger with the Sheikhs, who they saw as old-fashioned and reactionary, and in any case wanted to be rid of the British.

Student demonstrations escalated into riots and guerrilla outrage. Britain was determined to stay in Aden and so reinforced the garrison. A state of emergency was declared in 1963 and a full-scale counter-insurgency campaign began which was to last until the British granted independence and withdrew four years later.

Coups in Baghdad and Damascus

There was little stability elsewhere in the Arab world. Kassim's Iraq seethed with discontent and despite government repression the Ba'athist movement gained ground. In February 1963 Abdul Salam Aref and his Ba'athist allies instigated a successful coup. Unlike his one-time leader, Aref showed no mercy. General Kassim and many of his Marxist supporters were summarily executed.

A month later there was a coup in Damascus in which the Ba'athists were restored to power. The movement looked to its Pan-Arab heritage and a tripartite union between Egypt, Iraq and Syria.

However the Ba'athists could not accept Nasser as their leader, and because there was no other candidate of comparable stature, the idea was stillborn.

Despite chronic problems with the Egyptian economy and the Arabs in the Fertile Crescent and Arabia, Nasser's reputation continued to grow on the wider international scene. The rapid pace of decolonisation had brought many new states into the non-aligned camp. The death of Jawaharlal Nehru of India in 1964 elevated Nasser to the top rank of the movement's leadership alongside Tito of Yugoslavia and Fidel Castro of Cuba. But the problem of Israel was always in the background, threatening the Middle East with the prospect of war, and by the mid 1960s Nasser was forced to face the fact that any hopes he might have of maintaining his influence depended upon his ability to cope with the Jewish challenge. For there could be no doubt

that such a challenge existed, manifested in the continued growth and development of the Israeli Defence Forces (IDF) and their strategic thinking.

Israel's position

Such an emphasis upon the IDF is understandable in retrospect, for military success against the Egyptians in the Sinai Campaign of 1956 had done nothing to solve the fundamental problems of Israeli security. Potential enemies may have been deterred in the short term from attacking the Jewish state, but the war had produced neither recognition nor guarantees from surrounding Arab powers that still talked openly about the destruction of Israel.

The situation was not helped, in Israeli eyes, by the withdrawal (under international pressure) from Sinai and the Gaza Strip by March 1957, for this

marked a return to the unsatisfactory borders laid down at the 1949 ceasefire and left Israel extremely vulnerable to attack from a variety of quarters. In the north, Syrian artillery remained on the Golan Heights, dominating Jewish settlements in eastern Galilee, while the Lebanese continued to pose at least a potential threat. In the centre, Jordanian troops in Judea and Samaria overlooked the coastal strip and occupied high ground to the north of the Jerusalem corridor. Around Mount Scopus, to the east of Jerusalem, a small Jewish enclave even survived inside Jordanian territory.

In the south, despite the presence of a 3400-man United Nations Emergency Force, Egyptian troops were still in Sinai, threatening the Negev and the important port of Elat, while the Gaza Strip, containing Palestinian as well as Egyptian forces, pointed like a finger directly at Tel Aviv. Furthermore, as

Arab-Israeli forces – 1967			
country	men	tanks	aircraft
Israel	264,000	800	350
Egypt	240,000	1200	450
Syria	50,000	400	120
Jordan	50,000	200	40
Iraq	70,000	400	200
Saudi Arabia	50,000	100	20
Algeria	60,000	100	100
Kuwait	5000	24	9
Arab total	525,000	2424	939

Opposite: British soldiers in Aden search a loaded camel for any smuggled arms or explosives. Left: The Arab/Israeli military balance in 1967. Above: UAR troops in action in the North Yemen. Operations there were a great drain on Egyptian resources. Below: Muhammad al Badr (centre) who led the Royalist forces in North Yemen.

Israeli troops pulled out of Sharm el Sheikh in early 1957, Egypt regained control of the Straits of Tiran, the closure of which would cut Israel off from trading contacts to the south. In terms of geography alone, Israel was at a distinct disadvantage which she could not allow to become permanent.

Nor did the problem end there, for Israel also lacked the resources with which to match her Arab enemies. With a population of little over two million and a precarious economy, Israel could neither provide nor hope to sustain armed forces equal to those of her neighbours. By 1967 she could field a total of 264,000 service personnel (of which about 130,000 were front-line troops) against an estimated half a million Arabs (240,000 Egyptian, 50,000 Syrian, 50,000 Jordanian, 70,000 Iraqi, plus contingents from Saudi Arabia, Kuwait and other committed states). Even that figure would be hard to maintain for long, requiring a full mobilisation of reserves that would soon cripple the Israeli economy.

A similar imbalance applied to military equipment levels, especially after 1956 when the Soviet Union provided replacement weapons to Egypt and began to arm both Syria and Iraq. By the time of the Six Day War in 1967 the Israelis were in possession of about 800 tanks and 350 military aircraft, but they were facing Arab equivalents nearly three times as high – a total of over 2400 tanks (including 1200 Egyptian, 400 Syrian, 200 Jordanian and 400 Iraqi) and over 900 aircraft (including 450 Egyptian, 120 Syrian, 40 Jordanian and 200 Iraqi). Moreover, many of the Arab weapons, particularly the Soviet-supplied T–54/55 main battle tanks and MiG–21 interceptors of Egypt, Syria and Iraq, were among the most modern available. On the basis of these statistics, if the Arab powers ever came together to carry out their oft-repeated threat to destroy the state of Israel, there seemed little reason to doubt that they would be successful. Lacking the territorial depth to absorb an attack which could come from three directions simultaneously, and heavily outnumbered in both manpower and equipment, Israel appeared to be dangerously exposed.

The strategic balance

But in reality she did enjoy a number of advantages. The 1956 War and its immediate aftermath provided ample evidence that the superpowers were now involved in the Middle East, a develop-

ment which elevated the Arab-Israeli dispute from a regional to a global concern. This created a situation in which Israel's survival was likely to guaranteed, if only as a symbol of Western opposition to the spread of Soviet influence, and although this did not mean that Arab attacks would cease, it did ensure the imposition of international pressure, probably through the United Nations, to prevent a total Arab victory. Of course, the process would also work the other way, preventing the destruction of Arab states by Israel, but at least Israel would survive. At the same time the Sinai Campaign, providing an example of the ease with which the IDF could defeat its enemies, acted as a powerful deterrent to anything short of a concerted Arab attack, and that was unlikely to emerge easily. The political chaos that beset the Arab world for ten years after 1956 gave the Israelis a vital breathing space.

Israeli strategy

The Israelis used these advantages to perfect a strategy for survival. The first concern, as ever, was to prevent an Arab invasion; the second, reflecting the

recent growth of superpower interest in the Middle East, was to prepare for a short war in which decisive victories could be gained before international pressure forced a ceasefire. In neither case could the Israelis afford to adopt a strategy of passive defence; as the 1956 campaign had shown, the only way to remove a threat was to hit the enemy hard before he crossed into Israeli territory – a policy of offensive, pre-emptive military action. Between 1956 and 1967 this became the central core of Israeli thinking and the IDF was strengthened and modernised to reflect it, with special emphasis being placed upon armour and air power as the main components. New tanks were obtained – M-48 Pattons from West Germany and the United States, Centurions from Britain – and existing stocks of Shermans and AMX-13s were given new engines and up-gunned to create

Above: The new Israeli armour (M48s and Centurions) that were the core of the IDF by 1967. Below: King Hussein of Jordan and Nasser sign their 1967 agreement. Opposite above: The frontiers in 1967.

a fast-moving, hard-hitting armoured force that would be capable of repeating the blitzkrieg triumph of 1956 even against improved Arab armies.

At the same time, in order to ensure the protection of ground forces against air attack, the Israeli Air Force (IAF) was modernised and a balance of capability created. French-built Super Mystère and Mystère IVA fighter-bombers, backed by Vatour IIAs and Ouragans, would attack enemy airfields and rear-area locations while Mirage IIIJ interceptors swept enemy aircraft from the skies and provided cover for ground-attack machines such as the Fouga Magister. Some of the

new equipment had still to be delivered and deployed by 1967, but the IDF was undoubtedly a formidable force, making full use of the superior training, motivation and experience of Israeli soldiers to compensate the state for its geographical and numerical deficiencies.

The crisis develops

This was just as well, for when the crisis emerged that was to result in war in mid-1967, it did so slowly and unexpectedly, presenting Israel with exactly the sort of nightmare envisaged in the preparations for pre-emptive action. Arab attacks against Israel had never ceased altogether – Syrian artillery regularly shelled villages in eastern Galilee and, by the early 1960s, guerrilla raids by the Palestine Liberation Organisation (PLO) had become a familiar feature of Israeli life – but they were usually uncoordinated and easily contained, principally by a strategy of retaliatory cross-border raids by the IDF. Some Israeli successes had been achieved – in November 1964, for example, an Arab plan to deny water to northern Israel by diverting the Jordan River as it flowed through Syria was frustrated by the IAF, while a year later the destruction of

villages in Lebanon persuaded that country to reassess its policy towards the PLO – but almost inevitably, the scale of such confrontation gradually escalated. By November 1966 – by which time yet another coup had removed the Ba'athists from power in Damascus – Arab concern about Israeli actions and intentions led to the signing of a mutual defence pact between Egypt and Syria. At the same time President Nasser, prompted by the Soviet Union, began to make bitter speeches condemning both Israel and the United States. Syrian and PLO attacks in border areas intensified, which led in turn to stronger Israeli reprisals. On 13 November 1966, in one such retaliatory raid against PLO positions around the village of Samu in Jordan, 18 Jordanian soldiers were killed, and almost before the outcry over this had died down, two Egyptian MiG fighters were destroyed over Sinai. A more serious incident occurred on 7 April 1967, when Israeli forces, reacting to artillery attacks from the Golan Heights, were opposed by Syrian aircraft; the IAF was scrambled and in the ensuing dogfight six Syrian MiGs were shot down. The Egyptians made no move at this stage to support their ally, but the Soviets lodged strong protests in Tel Aviv

and began to circulate rumours of an Israeli build-up of forces on the Syrian border.

If the Soviet intention was to mobilise Arab opinion, the plan worked, for although the rumours turned out to be false, they were believed by Nasser, who decided that a show of force in Sinai might deter the Israelis by presenting the prospect of a war on two fronts while at the same time enhancing his own reputation as a Pan-Arab leader. On 14 May Egyptian forces began to cross the Suez Canal; within a week there were nearly 100,000 of them, organised into seven divisions and backed by an estimated 1000 tanks, deployed within striking distance of the Israeli frontier. To ensure freedom of movement, Nasser formally requested the United Nations to remove the Emergency Force and on 16 May Secretary-General U Thant rather tamely agreed.

The Israelis responded with a partial mobilisation of reservists and moved tanks and mechanised units into the Negev, but by this time the crisis was sliding out of control. Nasser, experiencing a wave of Pan-Arabism which had been absent for over a decade, began to receive offers of support from other Arab powers and, thus emboldened, took a crucial step towards inevitable war: on 22 May he closed the Straits of Tiran. Levy Eshkol, prime minister of Israel, tried to mobilise international pressure to defuse the situation but, with the Americans embroiled in Vietnam and the French surprisingly non-committal, all he succeeded in doing was to create an internal political crisis. This was only solved on 1 June when Moshe Dayan, the popular chief of staff of 1956, was appointed Minister of Defence. By then King Hussein had announced that Jordan would join the alliance against Israel, placing her forces under Egyptian command, and this completed the nightmare. Facing economic strangulation and the imminence of war on three fronts, Israel felt she had little choice but to initiate pre-emptive action. On 4 June – by which time the IDF had been fully mobilised – Dayan received Cabinet approval and ordered an attack for the next day. The third major Arab-Israeli conflict had begun.

6. The Six Day War

Once the decision had been made by the Israelis to initiate pre-emptive action against the Arab threat in June 1967, the first priority was to gain air supremacy. Without it, Israeli cities would be hostage to the bombing capabilities of Arab air forces and ground troops would be dangerously vulnerable as they advanced across the borders into enemy territory. On further analysis it was clear that the Egyptian Air Force posed the greatest threat, principally because of its size – about 370 interceptors and fighter-bombers (including 125 MiG–21F and 21PF supersonic fighters, believed to be more

than a match for Israeli aircraft, despite a combat radius of only 320km/200 miles) and 80 Ilyushin Il–28 and Tupolev Tu–16 bombers – but also because it was well placed to disrupt any Israeli moves into Sinai. Thus when Major-General Mordechai Hod, commanding the Israeli Air Force (IAF), was given the go-ahead late on 4 June, he unhesitatingly concentrated the bulk of his force – about 200 interceptors and fighter-bombers – against the Egyptians.

The attack was carefully planned to achieve maximum surprise. Israeli intelligence had discovered that, despite the

current political crisis, the Egyptians were still following a peace-time routine. They mounted dawn air patrols but depended heavily upon radar stations to provide warning of an Israeli attack and expected their Soviet-supplied anti-aircraft defences – 150 SA–2 missiles, deployed in 25 six-launcher batteries in a band on either side of the Suez Canal – to inflict telling damage. If the attack could be launched after the dawn patrols had returned to base and could somehow avoid both radar and surface-to-air missile (SAM) defences, the Egyptians would be helpless. For these reasons Hod directed his first wave of 40

Mystères, protected by a similar number of Mirages, to fly low and fast against four airfields in Sinai (El Arish, Jebel Libni, Bir Thimada and Bir Gifgafa) and to bypass the east-facing defences of a further five (Fayid and Kabrit on the Suez Canal, Abu Sueir in the Delta region, Beni Sueif on the Nile and Cairo West) by approaching them from the Mediterranean. They were to arrive at precisely 0745 (0845 Egyptian time) on 5 June, at a time when it was known little air activity would be taking place.

Air strike at dawn

It worked perfectly. As the morning mists cleared, the Mystères and Mirages swept down out of a clear sky to find Egyptian aircraft lined up in neat rows on the runways, as if awaiting inspection. Each Israeli pilot had fuel for exactly ten minutes over his target, sufficient time to make three or four passes, and none wasted the opportunity to inflict maximum damage. Dropping bombs – including rocket-assisted 'Concrete Dibbers' designed to penetrate hardened surfaces – onto runways and airfield facilities on the first run, the Mystères then circled back to rake the enemy aircraft with cannon-fire. By the time they turned for home, a second wave was already arriving, to be followed at ten-minute intervals by a further three until,

after an incredibly quick refuelling and rearming 'turn round' (reduced in some cases to as little as seven or eight minutes) the first wave was ready to return.

This continued for 80 minutes until 0905, only to start again ten minutes later, initially against the same nine airfields but, after three-quarters of an hour, against a further three (El Mansura and Helwan in the Delta and El Minya on the Nile). Another pause occurred between 1035 and noon, as the IAF reformed, and thereafter the pace slackened significantly. Even so, a further five airfields (Bilbeis, Hurqhada, Luxor, El Banas and Cairo International) had been hit by nightfall. The results were devastating:

Opposite: The strain shows on the face of this young Israeli soldier during close-quarters fighting in the Six Day War. Above and below: Mirage fighters of the type that ruled the skies in 1967.

Above: A Mirage in combat with an Egyptian aircraft. Air superiority was the key to Israeli success in 1967.

by the end of the day the Egyptians had lost all 30 of their Tu–16s, 27 Il–28s, 12 Sukhoi Su–7 fighter-bombers, 90 MiG–21s, 20 MiG–19 and 25 MiG–17 fighters and 32 transports and helicopters. For the loss of 19 of their own aircraft – all to ground-fire – the Israelis had effectively wiped out the largest and potentially the most dangerous air force in the Middle East.

Disaster for Jordan

Nor was this the end of the story, for at about 1100 on 5 June, King Hussein, mistakenly believing that the Egyptians were winning the air war, ordered his meagre force of 22 British-built Hawker Hunter ground-attack fighters to assault Israeli targets. This they did, dropping bombs on Nathanya as well as airfields at Kfar Sava and Kfar Sirkin before returning unharmed to Jordan. The Israeli reaction was swift and ruthless: at 1215 Mirages attacked the Jordanian airfields at Mafraq and Amman, pouring cannon-fire into the Hunters as they were being refuelled, before sweeping round to drop bombs onto runways and service areas. Twenty minutes later, the Royal Jordanian Air Force had ceased to exist: for

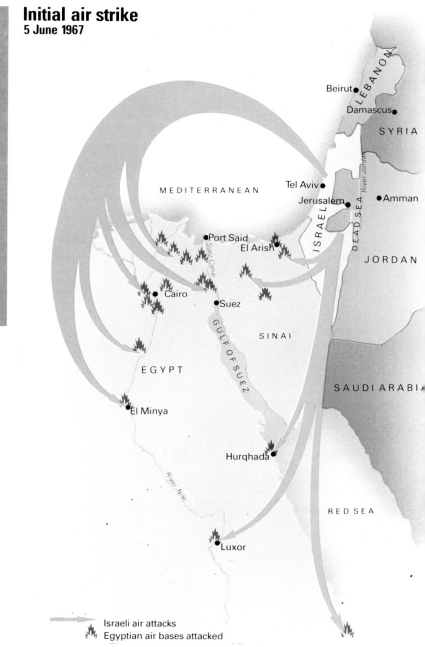

Initial air strike
5 June 1967

→ Israeli air attacks
Egyptian air bases attacked

Above: The first air strike. Opposite above: Egyptian aircraft lie destroyed on their runway. Below: A Syrian MiG–21 hit by a Mirage. Opposite below: Israelis inspect a captured Soviet-built SA-2 missile.

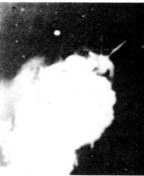

the loss of only one Mirage (the pilot of which ejected over friendly territory) the IAF had destroyed 18 of the Hunters and severely damaged the other four.

A similar pattern of events affected the Syrians who, despite their rhetoric and propaganda, initially made no move to attack Israel on 5 June. But at 1145, intent upon participation in a war which the Egyptians boasted they were winning, 12 Syrian MiG–21s dropped bombs on Haifa and around Tiberias in northern Israel. Half an hour later, coinciding with the raids on Jordan, Israeli Mystères attacked four airfields in Syria (Damascus, Marj Rial, Seikel and a desert station known simply as 'T–4'). All returned safely, leaving behind the burning wrecks of 32 MiG–21s, 23 MiG–15 and MiG–17 fighters and two Il–28 bombers, a tally that constituted about two-thirds of the effective Syrian Air Force.

This left only one conceivable threat – the numerically strong Iraqi Air Force – and this was ignored until 6 June, when a single raid against the only airfield within range of Israel ('H–3') destroyed nine aircraft for no Israeli loss. By then Israeli control of the air was undeniably

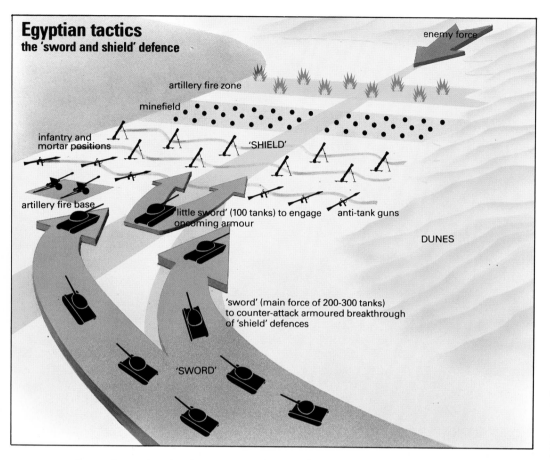

Egyptian tactics
the 'sword and shield' defence

enemy force

artillery fire zone

minefield

infantry and
mortar positions

'SHIELD'

artillery fire base

'little sword' (100 tanks) to engage
oncoming armour

anti-tank guns

DUNES

'sword' (main force of 200-300 tanks)
to counter-attack armoured breakthrough
of 'shield' defences

'SWORD'

thening their defences. They concentrated on the two main routes across the difficult terrain of Sinai – that in the north between Gaza and Qantara and the one in the centre between Nitzana and Ismailiya – with the aim of denying to the Israelis any opportunity to move freely or to repeat the blitzkrieg-style advance of 1956. The main roads were resurfaced, lateral routes were established to connect the northern and central axes and a new Pass (the Giddi) was opened through the western mountains, parallel to the Mitla – all designed to enhance the flexibility of Egyptian forces. At the same time complex defensive locations were built astride the main routes – around Rafah and El Arish in the north and at Abu Aweigila and Um Qataf in the centre – and the Gaza Strip was transformed into a fortress, with dug-in tanks and artillery covering all the likely approaches. By June 1967, with seven Egyptian divisions deployed to exploit the natural and manmade features of the region, Sinai appeared to be impervious to attack and a launch-pad for an invasion of Israel.

Sword and shield

In defensive terms, Egyptian tactics were based on the Soviet concept of 'sword and shield'. A total of five infantry divisions constituted the 'shield', occupying fortified locations close to the Israeli border or astride the likely routes of advance: the 20th (Palestinian) in the Gaza Strip, the 7th around Rafah and El Arish, the 2nd in the area from Quseima to Abu Aweigila (in which was included the Um Qataf stronghold), the 3rd around Jebel Libni and Bir Hassana, and the 6th (Mechanised) astride the Kuntilla-Nakhl axis. Their task was to halt Israeli armour by enmeshing it in minefields, anti-tank traps and pre-set artillery fire zones, giving time for the 'sword' to react. This sword was provided by two armoured formations – the 4th Armoured Division, concentrated around Bir Gifgafa and Bir Thimada in central Sinai, and the so-called Shazli Force (commanded by Major-General Saad el Din Shazli, who was to be chief of staff to the Egyptian Army at the time of the Yom Kippur War of 1973) between Quseima

complete: altogether in the pre-emptive air strikes of 5 June, over 300 Arab aircraft had been destroyed (most of them on the ground) for the loss of 20 Israeli machines. It was a notable and far-reaching victory.

It had been an enormous gamble, however. Israel committed almost her entire front-line air strength to the attacks – on 5 June only 12 Super Mystères were kept back to protect the homeland – and if success had not been achieved, the war would have taken an entirely different course, particularly after it widened out to involve both the Jordanians and Syrians. In the event, however, the gamble paid off and by mid-day on 5 June elements of the IAF were already being diverted to ground support as the second phase of Israel's offensive against Egypt – an armoured assault on Sinai – took shape.

Planning the ground attack

The initial plan, discussed by the Israeli Cabinet in late May, envisaged a limited armoured drive into northern Sinai, designed to disrupt Egyptian preparations for an invasion of Israel and to gain territory which would later be exchanged,

after the inevitable United Nations ceasefire, for a re-opening of the Straits of Tiran. This was quickly altered by Dayan when he became Minister of Defence on 1 June, for he recognised its potential dangers. If the Israelis confined their attacks in this way they would not only be pitting themselves against the most heavily defended Egyptian positions, around Rafah and El Arish and in the Gaza Strip, but would also leave themselves extremely vulnerable to counter-attack by those enemy forces unaffected by the initial fighting. In addition, the Egyptians might well refuse to re-open the Straits, depending upon international pressure to restore the territorial status quo, as had happened in 1956. According to Dayan, the only sure way to achieve lasting security was to destroy the Egyptian Army entirely, take Sinai as a buffer and control the Straits of Tiran through permanent occupation of their western shores. With the Egyptian Air Force rendered ineffective, this was now within the realms of possibility.

Even so, the task in 1967 was a formidable one, for the Egyptians had spent the intervening years improving and streng-

and Kuntilla – which would use the improved roads of the area to mount counter-attacks into the flanks of the stalled Israelis. In theory this seemed flawless, but in practice it had its weaknesses. Despite the new lateral communications, gaps still existed in areas where the terrain was thought by the Egyptians to be impassable; cooperation between infantry and armour was poor; many units, having taken up their positions as recently as the last week in May, had not settled in and, of course, no account had been taken of a sudden loss of air support. It was enough to give the Israelis a chance of victory.

Responsibility for carrying out the Sinai attack lay with the Israeli Southern Command, under Major-General Yeshayahu Gavish. On 5 June he had three divisions available, commanded respectively by Major-Generals Israel Tal, Avraham Yoffe and Ariel Sharon, fielding a total of about 700 tanks, supported by mechanized infantry and artillery. They were concentrated between Nitzana and the Mediterranean coast – a distance of about 65km (40 miles) – and their task was to destroy the superior Egyptian forces facing them on the northern and central trans-Sinai routes, preparatory to a complete occupation of the region.

The attack was to be in two broad phases. As the bulk of the Egyptian infantry was well forward, close to the Israeli border, the first priority was to break through or bypass their defensive strongholds, destroying the 'shield' and opening the way for more mobile operations. These would constitute the second phase, in which rapid armoured thrusts deep into Sinai along the northern and central axes would disrupt and destroy the Egyptian armoured 'sword'. Quite how this was to be achieved in detail was not finalised until 6 June, when a supplementary 'phase' was added. This entailed the advance of Israeli armour through the enemy's confusion to seal the eastern end of the Mitla and Giddi Passes, blocking the Egyptian line of retreat and squeezing his remaining forces between Israeli units in the west and advancing formations from the east. It was classic blitzkrieg, involving an initial breakthrough, followed swiftly by rear-area disruption, demoralisation and collapse.

The tanks go in

The attack began at 0800 on 5 June, soon after the first of the pre-emptive air strikes had been delivered, and was concentrated on the northern axis around Rafah and El Arish. One of Tal's brigades – the 7th Armoured, commanded by Colonel Shmuel Gonen – advanced through the thin line of enemy defences on the border to the north-east of Rafah, close to the town of Khan Yunis and along the interface between the 7th (Egyptian) and 20th (Palestinian) Divisions. Gonen's objective was the defensive stronghold around Rafah, the occupation

The battle for Sinai

5 June 1967
6 June 1967
7 June 1967
8 June 1967

Opposite: The basic Egyptian defensive system. Above: The Israeli advances into Sinai. Below: Israeli troops with jeep-mounted recoilless rifles after an engagement.

of which would cut off the Gaza Strip and open the road, through El Arish, to Qantara. His M–48s and Centurions initially intended to skirt the Khan Yunis defences, aiming directly for the main road close to the coast (which was in constant use and therefore unlikely to be mined) before turning westwards. But they soon came under heavy artillery fire from the direction of Khan Yunis and encountered line after line of minefields, trenches and artillery fire-zones to the east of Rafah. As casualties mounted, the thin corridor of advance began to look like a potential death-trap.

Gonen reacted quickly. Diverting his Centurion battalion to take Khan Yunis, thus silencing enemy fire from his right, he ordered his M–48s to break through towards Rafah 'regardless of cost'. Fouga Magister ground-attack aircraft were used to lay down suppressive fire and individual Egyptian positions were taken out at long range by expert Israeli tank gunners. Meanwhile, the second of Tal's brigades – 'P' Paratroop, commanded by Colonel Rafael ('Raful') Eitan, the hero of Parker's Memorial in 1956 – crossed the border at Nitzana and moved along a disused road to assault Rafah from the south. The paras found the going hard

but their sudden appearance, together with the fall of Khan Yunis to the east, probably diverted Egyptian attention sufficiently to allow Gonen's Brigade Battle Reserve of Centurions to push through to the coastal road. Once on it, the tanks turned left and gradually picked up speed, firing on Egyptian defenders as they went. By mid-afternoon they had covered 48km (30 miles) and were at the outskirts of El Arish. Unfortunately, as soon as they had passed along the road, the Egyptians emerged from their shelters and blocked the way for follow-up units, particularly at Jiradi, where a narrow pass made defence a relatively easy task.

Tal, recognising the danger, ordered his third brigade – 'M' Armoured, commanded by Colonel M. Aviram and equipped with AMX–13s and Shermans – to swing through the desert, avoiding Rafah, and attack the Jiradi positions from the south. But the light tanks soon bogged down in soft sand and, as Eitan's paras began to call for assistance, the bulk of the brigade was diverted to Rafah. The link-up with the Centurions at El Arish had therefore to be undertaken by Gonen alone and it was only after a series of bitter and costly frontal assaults that the Jiradi Pass was cleared.

Above: The mass of Egyptian equipment abandoned in Sinai during the headlong retreat. Below and opposite below: The Centurion was one of the mainstays of Israeli armoured strength, its thick hull armour, good interior design and excellent gun making it more than a match for the best Arab tank, the T-54/55.

T54
weight 36 tonnes (35.4 tons)
length 9.02 (29ft 7in) **height**
2.68m (8ft 9½in) **armament**
1 x 100mm gun, 2 x 7.62mm
and 1 x 12.7mm machine guns
ammunition carried 42 rounds of
APHE, HEAT and HE, 3000 rounds
for 7.62mm, 500 rounds for
12.7mm

Centurion V
weight 51.8 tonnes (51 tons)
length 9.85m (32ft 4in)
height 3m (9ft 10½in)
armament 1 x 105mm gun,
2 x 7.62mm and 1 x 12.7mm
machine guns **ammunition
carried** 64 rounds APDS and
HESH, 4250 rounds for
7.62mm, 700 rounds 12.7mm

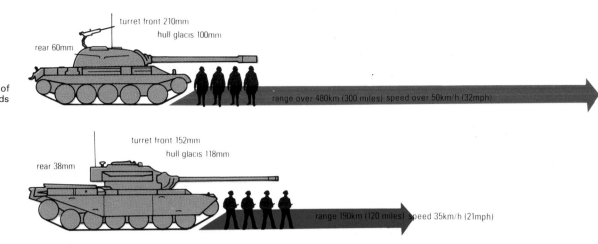

turret front 210mm
hull glacis 100mm
rear 60mm
range over 480km (300 miles) speed over 50km/h (32mph)

turret front 152mm
hull glacis 118mm
rear 38mm
range 190km (120 miles) speed 35km/h (21mph)

By now it was early evening and fighting was still going on in Rafah itself as well as around Khan Yunis, where Palestinian resistance had unexpectedly hardened. Nevertheless, for the loss of 70 men and 34 tanks, Tal had broken through an extremely deep defensive line in about 12 hours and this rapidity persuaded the hapless defenders of El Arish to offer little resistance when Gonen's brigade attacked them early on 6 June. With an infantry brigade, supported by Eitan's paras, detailed to clear the Gaza Strip – a difficult process which was to take until noon on 7 June – the northern route lay open.

Sharon's attack in the south

While all this was going on, Sharon's division to the south was concentrating on the central Nitzana – Ismailiya axis, a vital route containing roads not just to the west but also to El Arish in the north and Nakhl in the south. But the Abu Aweigila and Um Qataf position, held by the Egyptian 2nd Division together with a force of 66 T–34 tanks and 22 Su–100 tank destroyers, lay like a huge rock barring the way. It was essential that this be destroyed. Sharon initially favoured a surprise frontal assault along the main road, using his one armoured brigade to break through, followed closely by his infantry, before the enemy could react. But when the Centurions and Shermans crossed the border at 0840 on 5 June they encountered so much opposition from artillery and mines that the situation had to be reassessed.

On analysis, the Um Qataf position contained a basic flaw, for despite the existence of some outlying defences, all the trench lines and minefields faced eastwards, towards the Israeli frontier. They rested to north and south on what appeared to be strong natural features – a sand-sea and a low rocky massif (the Jebel Dalfa) respectively – and the terrain all around was believed by the Egyptians to be impassable to armoured units. But if Sharon could manoeuvre forces into positions on both flanks, he could turn his troops inwards and roll up the enemy lines. With this in mind, he spent the rest of the daylight hours of 5 June bringing up his division, concentrating six battalions of artillery to the east of Um Qataf and sending armoured reconnaissance units to north and south to surround the stronghold and cut it off from all outside reinforcement. As dusk fell, an infantry brigade struggled through soft sand to positions directly north of the Egyptian trench lines and a paratroop battalion was lifted by helicopter into sand dunes to the north of the enemy artillery park, which was situated well back and virtually unprotected. H-Hour was set for 2330.

Centurion versus T-34

At 2245 the Israeli artillery, quiet during the day, suddenly opened up with a massive barrage and, three-quarters of an hour later, the infantry and paras attacked. The artillery park proved to be vulnerable and although bitter hand-to-hand fighting took place, the Egyptians were swiftly denied the bulk of their fire support. This certainly helped the infantry, who began to roll up the forward trenches from the north. As soon as the first section had been captured, engineers

Above: Egyptian troops in Sinai just before the main Israeli attack. Although well-equipped by the Soviet Union, the Egyptian Army was inferior to the Israeli Defence Force in the training of its men, and suffered from its lack of air cover.

rushed forward to clear the minefields and this allowed the armour, pinned down since early morning, to advance into Um Qataf. At the same time the armoured reconnaissance units, sitting astride the roads leading into the stronghold, turned inwards and attacked. An armoured battle developed, but the T–34s and Su–100s were no match for Sharon's Centurions. By 0600 on 6 June Israeli forces had linked up in the centre of Umm Qataf and, although fighting was to continue throughout the day as the last pockets of resistance were cleared, the central trans-Sinai route now lay exposed and open.

One of the factors which undoubtedly helped Tal and Sharon to achieve their objectives was that while they were fighting their battles Yoffe's division was advancing across the 'impassable' terrain between the northern and central routes, cutting lateral communications and blocking the movement of Egyptian reinforcements. The task was by no means easy,

Opposite below: An Israeli tankman, 0.5 inch Browning machine-gun at the ready, looks across the border into Jordan, the country that was to suffer the most from the Six Day War. Above: The crew of an Israeli Centurion take a short break.

with heavy Centurions crawling slowly across a series of sand ridges to the north-west of Nitzana, but by nightfall on 5 June 'I' Armoured Brigade, commanded by Colonel Yiska Shadmi, had managed to penetrate about 55km (35 miles) to a road junction south of Bir Lahfan on the route which Egyptian armour would be forced to use if it moved towards El Arish.

Shadmi had encountered little resistance in his advance and once in place he was able to deploy his tanks in hull-down ambush positions, confident that the enemy was not aware of his move. He was rewarded at about 2100 when two Egyptian brigades – one armoured and one mechanised – suddenly appeared, heading north up the El Arish road. They were engaged at once, initiating an armoured battle which was to continue throughout the night, but by dawn on 6 June the Egyptians had had enough. They withdrew, leaving Shadmi in secure possession of one of the most important

lateral communication routes in eastern Sinai. The Egyptian 'shield' had been well and truly penetrated and the first 'sword' reaction had been blunted, all within 24 hours of the beginning of the war.

Gavish called his divisional commanders together on 6 June to discuss the next move, and it was at this meeting that the decision was made to advance through Egyptian lines to block off the western escape routes. This was put forward as part of an overall plan of pursuit and the task divided between Tal and Yoffe, the former to concentrate on the route Bir Gifgafa – Ismailiya and the latter on the Mitla and Giddi Passes. Sharon was to complete the clearance of Um Qataf before striking south-westwards to take Nakhl, a move which would threaten the rear of Shazli Force, still deployed close to the Israeli border, and persuade it to withdraw to the west, into the trap created by Tal and Yoffe.

With the IAF now available to provide almost unlimited air support, particularly in the process of blocking the western passes, the Egyptians were about to be out-manoeuvred, but this did not mean that the fighting was over. A substantial proportion of the Egyptian Army in Sinai – the 3rd Division at Jebel Libni, 6th (Mechanised) at Nakhl and 4th Ar-

moured around Bir Gifgafa, plus Shazli Force between Quseima and Kuntilla – was still intact, posing a potential threat that had to be removed.

Laying the traps

These Egyptian deployments dictated the detail of the subsequent Israeli advance. In the north Tal continued to push directly towards the Suez Canal, sending his reconnaissance units under Colonel Israel Granit along the road to Qantara (the town was to fall on 8 June after a bitter tank battle in the desert approaches), but he diverted the bulk of his armour – 7th and 'M' Brigades – south to Bir Lahfan on 6 June. There they linked up with Colonel Shadmi of Yoffe's division before moving south-westwards towards Jebel Libni. The aim was to trap the Egyptian 3rd Division, but they withdrew before contact could be made, leaving small rearguards that were swiftly overcome. A new objective was immediately laid down. While Tal aimed directly for Bir Gifgafa, Yoffe swung his main force south to Bir Hassana and Bir Thimada in a wide encircling move designed to trap the Egyptian 4th Armoured Division in a huge 'killing zone'. Once again, however, the Egyptians

Egyptian infantry digging in in Sinai, preparing to meet the Israeli attack.

declined to give battle, enabling Tal to occupy Bir Gifgafa on 7 June, and although a force of 60 T–54/55s did attempt a counter-attack early on the 8th, this was defeated. By daylight on 8 June Tal was able to order a broad advance, against minimal opposition, to the Suez Canal. He re-established his links with both Granit in the north and Yoffe in the south on the banks of the Canal early on the 9th.

Meanwhile Yoffe had continued through Bir Thimada on 7 June and, when the projected encirclement of 4th Armoured failed, he concentrated upon taking the Mitla and Giddi Passes. In accordance with the revised strategy of 6 June, elements of his division, spearheaded from Jebel Libni by Shadmi's Centurions, rushed ahead to exploit Egyptian confusion. Their task was not easy. The roads were packed with retreating enemy units, the IAF was attacking anything that moved and supply lines were impossible to maintain. As a result, although Shadmi pushed through to block the eastern end of the Mitla Pass by the evening of 7 June, he did so with only nine Centurions, and four of those, their fuel tanks dry, were under tow. Nevertheless their arrival had an effect out of all proportion to their strength, for it dealt a stunning psychological blow to enemy soldiers already reeling from the rush of recent events.

Through the night of 7/8 June, as Shadmi's small force successfully blocked the approaches to the Pass, remaining Egyptian units in Sinai lost all cohesion, convinced that the Israelis had pushed major formations as far as the Suez Canal. Shadmi held out until the morning, destroying anything that came within range of his guns, and when the rest of the division linked up early on the 8th, the equivalent of an entire enemy tank battalion lay in ruins before him.

Yoffe found that all organised resistance was coming to an end – an attempted counter-attack by 30 Egyptian tanks, supported by the remnants of their air force, at noon on 8 June constituted the last engagement of the war in this sector – and he advanced through both the Mitla and Giddi Passes during the day. His troops were presented with an awe-inspiring sight, for the IAF had turned the Passes into avenues of destruction: hundreds, if not thousands, of enemy vehicles lay shattered or abandoned. Yoffe detached a small force southwestwards to support a para-drop that took Ras Sudar on the coast of the Gulf of Suez late on 8 June and halted his division on the banks of the Canal to await the arrival of Tal.

The tanks destroyed by Shadmi on 7/8 June probably belonged in part to Shazli Force, for while battles were taking place around the Passes, the southern sector of Egyptian defences had been unhinged by Sharon. After spending 6 June mopping-up around Um Qataf, he advanced south towards Nakhl, hoping to outflank Shazli and destroy the positions occupied by the 6th (Mechanised) Division. At the same time a fresh Israeli brigade moved across the border at Kuntilla and this was enough to persuade Shazli to withdraw, away from a rapidly developing trap. He did so without liaising with 6th (Mechanised), the main force of which, lacking its 'sword' protection, was caught and annihilated by Sharon on 7 June.

This left the whole of southern Sinai denuded of Egyptian forces, enabling Israeli gun-boats and paras to capture Sharm el Sheikh without firing a shot. They secured the port and moved quickly up the west coast of Sinai to make contact with Yoffe's detachment at Ras Sudar, a process completed late on 8 June. Sharon, meanwhile, advanced out of Nakhl towards Bir Thimada, joining forces with Yoffe in the push through the Passes.

The ceasefire in Sinai

A United Nations ceasefire was accepted by both sides on 9 June and this marked the end of the Sinai Campaign of 1967. All three of Dayan's pre-war objectives had been secured: Sinai had been captured, Sharm el Sheikh and the Straits of Tiran were in Israeli hands and a large, well-equipped Egyptian Army had been routed – all in four days. The Israelis lost a reported 300 dead and about 1000 wounded during the campaign, but they had inflicted terrible damage. An estimated 15,000 Egyptians died – many of thirst as they roamed leaderless and lost in the desert areas of Sinai after the battles were over – and although most of the remainder were allowed to escape across the Canal by Israelis who lacked the facilities for vast numbers of POWs, they left the bulk of their equipment behind.

Sinai was littered with over 800 Egyptian tanks – many of them still intact – and up to 10,000 military vehicles and heavy weapons, including artillery pieces and at least one complete SA–2 battery. Nasser himself was later to admit that his forces had suffered 80% equipment loss. It was a comprehensive defeat.

But Egypt constituted only part of the threat facing Israel in June 1967, for while the battles were raging in Sinai, the war was escalating elsewhere. When the decision to initiate pre-emptive action was taken on 4 June, the Israelis were probably hoping that the attack on Egypt would be sufficient to deter other Arab states, at least until the objectives of the Sinai Campaign had been achieved. In the case of both Lebanon and (initially) Syria this seems to have worked – on 5 June, despite presidential orders, the Lebanese armed forces refused to move against northern Israel, while the Syrians contented themselves with sporadic air and artillery strikes, even after their airfields had been hit – but this was not so with Jordan.

The Jordanian intervention

King Hussein, wary of becoming isolated in a potentially hostile Arab world and convinced by Nasser's assurances that Israel was about to be destroyed, ordered his forces to attack Israeli positions at 1100 on 5 June. Long-range 155mm artillery, sited in the hills overlooking the coastal strip, opened up against Tel Aviv, Lydda (Lod) and Ramat Dawid, air strikes hit Nathanya, Kfar Sava and Kfar Sirkin, and firing broke out in Jerusalem. Prime Minister Eshkol, acutely aware of the vulnerability of Israeli positions – along the coast, in the Jerusalem Corridor and around Jerusalem itself – tried to prevent the development of full-scale war by sending messages of assurance to Amman, but to no avail. Caught up in the prevailing mood of Arab hysteria, Hussein was determined to contribute to the destruction of Israel.

It is easy to see why Eshkol was so concerned, for the IDF was neither prepared nor deployed for a war against Jordan. Most of the first-line Israeli units had been committed to the Sinai attack, leaving the Central and Northern Commands, under Major-General Uzi Narkiss and Colonel David Elazar respectively, understrength and dependent upon reservists. Narkiss was responsible for defending the Jewish areas of Jerusalem and the corridor leading to the city as well as for keeping a watch on southern Samaria and the whole of Judea, yet he had just three infantry brigades available. In the north, Elazar was theoretically better off, commanding one armoured and six infantry brigades, but he was responsible for the borders with Lebanon and Syria as well as northern Samaria. Some units were held in reserve – the 10th 'Harel' Mechanised Brigade under Colonel Uri Ben Ari in the centre and an armoured division under Major-General Elad Peled in the north – but they represented the last of the IDF formations available in June 1967 and could never be committed to a campaign against Jordan without taking an enormous gamble on the borders with Lebanon and Syria.

The Eastern fronts – Jordan and Syria

Hussein's army

By comparison the Jordanians seemed to be numerically strong and strategically well-placed. The majority of Hussein's army – seven infantry and two armoured brigades – was deployed on the West Bank, occupying good defensive positions in mountainous terrain. In the

Above: The Syrians and Jordanians were to suffer badly as Israeli victory in Sinai left them very vulnerable to the IDF. Below: Shermans of the IDF, up-gunned and up-armoured during the 1960s, move into enemy territory during the advance into Jordanian areas.

north two infantry brigades controlled the Jenin – Nablus – Tulkarem triangle, while a third was dug in between Latrun and Ramallah on high ground overlooking the Jerusalem Corridor. Two more were stationed in and around Jerusalem itself, with a sixth held back around Jericho as a reserve. The seventh was in Judea, strung out among the Hebron Hills to the south of Bethlehem. They were supported by two armoured brigades, equipped largely with M–48s – the 40th, concentrated around the Damiya Bridge on the Jordan River, available for movement into Samaria, and the 60th at Jericho, ready to support either Jerusalem or a drive through Judea into the Negev.

In addition, by 5 June an Egyptian commando unit had reinforced the Latrun Salient, an Iraqi infantry brigade had arrived in Jordan as the spearhead of a much larger force, Saudi Arabian troops had moved up to the Jordanian border and the Syrians had promised to launch an attack in the north to draw Elazar's forces away from Samaria. Little wonder, therefore, that Hussein felt confident enough, at 1300 on 5 June, to step up his military action, increasing the weight

of artillery fire all along the front line, moving elements of 40th Armoured Brigade forward towards Nablus and sending units of his Arab Legion into the United Nations demilitarised zone around Government House to the south of the Old City of Jerusalem.

The initial Israeli reaction was positive although, of necessity, improvised. The occupation of Government House posed an obvious threat, for it seemed to be the first move in a Jordanian attempt to encircle the Jewish Quarter of the city, and Narkiss wasted no time in mounting a local counter-attack. By this time the Jordanian Air Force had ceased to exist, so when reservists of the 16th Infantry Brigade began their advance at 1430 they did so without fear of air attack and quickly pushed the Jordanians back. They were so successful, in fact, that they continued beyond their objective as far as the village of Zur Baher. As this lay astride the main Jerusalem–Hebron road, cutting Jordanian contact with the infantry brigade in Judea, an enemy reaction became inevitable. Whether they liked it or not, the Israelis would now have to fight a major campaign on the West Bank.

War on the West Bank

Contingency plans for a war against Jordan already existed, but with the prevailing situation in Sinai and the lack of readily available forces, the ensuing Israeli attack was to a large extent extemporised. In the north Peled's division was ordered to advance into Samaria to defeat Jordanian forces around Jenin before fanning out eastwards to the Jordan River and south to Nablus; in the south Narkiss was to secure the Jerusalem Corridor, establish contact with the Mount Scopus enclave and push north to link up with Peled. As in Sinai, the intention was to break through enemy forward defences before advancing in broad encircling moves to trap reserve formations and cut off lines of retreat.

Narkiss moved first, sending Ben Ari's mechanised brigade to clear the high ground to the north of the Jerusalem Corridor, on the line Latrun–Ramallah. Ben Ari, given little time for preparation or reconnaissance, improvised his attack, driving towards Jerusalem before suddenly turning his force, in three parallel columns, into the hills. The Jordanians were taken by surprise and although the fighting was bitter, with Israeli tanks destroying enemy fortifications at point-blank range, by 1730 on 5 June Ben Ari's men had penetrated as far as Abdul Aziz, Radar Hill and Beit Itsa. This broke the Jordanian line, enabling the Israelis to push north and east onto high ground overlooking the key road junction at Ramallah. By dawn on 6 June they had been joined by infantry units that had assaulted and cleared the Latrun Salient and the Jerusalem Corridor was freed from the danger of attack.

Above left: Israeli reservists march up to the front near Jerusalem, as the fighting for the city intensifies. Left: the breakthrough into Jordanian territory, a column of Centurions halts for a moment. Opposite: Moment of triumph for Defence Minister Moshe Dayan as he enters Bethlehem.

But this was only a preliminary, for as the fighting escalated the Israelis became justifiably concerned about the security of Jewish enclaves in and around Jerusalem itself. During the afternoon of 5 June the decision was taken to attack to the north of the Old City, with the aim of re-establishing contact with the Mount Scopus position, surrounded since the ceasefire of 1949 and now under renewed threat. To carry out the task, Narkiss was given 55th Paratroop Brigade, an élite formation commanded by Colonel Mor-dechai ('Motta') Gur that had suddenly become available as a projected para-drop on El Arish in Sinai ceased to be essential. The paras moved to Central Command late on 5 June, with no time for detailed briefings, and were ordered to push through the Sheikh Jarrach area to the north of Jerusalem, link up with Mount Scopus and take high ground to the south along the Augusta Victoria Hill and Mount of Olives before establishing con-tact with 16th Infantry Brigade around Zur Baher. At this stage there were no direct orders to capture the Old City and its holy shrines, but the overall intention was to encircle Jordanian posi-tions in that area and make them unten-able. As the paras moved up to their start-line the IAF interdicted the road to Jericho, preventing the movement of Jordanian infantry and armour reinforce-ments.

The paras go in

Gur's attack began just before midnight on 5/6 June, entering built-up areas which the Jordanians had spent nearly 20 years protecting and fortifying. The fighting was hard – especially for Ammu-nition Hill on the left flank – and went on under the glare of Israeli searchlights, for four hours before the Jordanian Arab Legion troops, unsupported by forces from Jericho, began to withdraw. Gur used the last of his reserves to push through Sheikh Jarrach towards the Rockefeller Museum, clearing the area immediately to the north of the Old City, close to the Damascus Gate. Contact was made with Mount Scopus, while further north Ben Ari advanced to cut the road from Ramallah and isolate Jerusalem from Jordanian forces in Samaria.

The Israelis now paused, partly because of United Nations pressure for a cease-fire and partly because no-one was willing to take the next logical step and attack the Old City itself for fear of damaging the holy shrines. It was not until 0830 on 7 June that Gur was authorised to con-tinue his advance and even then he was not permitted to use artillery or tank fire within the confines of the Old City wall. However, his first concern was to con-solidate his existing positions, so his initial move was towards the Augusta Victoria Hill. This was captured in a two-pronged attack with heavy air and artil-lery support, enabling the paras to push south to the Mount of Olives and into the Qidron Valley, where they linked up with 16th Infantry Brigade.

The road to Jericho was now com-pletely severed, forcing the Jordanians to withdraw, and this left the Old City virtually undefended. Gur led the way through St Stephen's (Lion's) Gate and at 1000 on 7 June his paras, advancing cautiously because of sporadic sniper fire, took the holiest of Jewish shrines – the Wailing Wall. As they continued to clear the rest of the bity, 16th Infantry Brigade pushed south into Judea, taking Bethle-hem, Etzion and Hebron in quick suc-cession. They linked up with Israeli forces in Sinai early on 8 June. So far, all was going well for the Israelis.

Meanwhile, in the north, Peled had fought a series of difficult battles in the

Above: The fighting on the Golan Heights was severe. Here, Shermans of the IDF go into the attack. Below: M13 half-tracks on their way to reinforce the Israeli front-line troops. Bottom: An AMX-13 light tank during the fighting on Golan. Opposite above: The basic Israeli method of attack was to punch a hole with armour, and then push on, leaving mechanised infantry to mop up and ensure that supplies reached the leading units.

mountainous terrain of Samaria. Crossing the border at 1700 on 5 June, he deployed two brigades to the west of Jenin with the intention of taking high ground to the south before capturing the town. A small diversionary assault down the Beit Shean Valley to the east was designed to tie down Jordanian armour, but in the event it was already too late. Elements of 40th Armoured Brigade had moved up to Nablus earlier on 5 June and, although Peled encircled and captured Jenin within 24 hours, he had suddenly to redeploy his tanks to the south of the town, around Kabatiya in the Dotan Valley, to deal with a further advance by the Jordanian M–48s. The Israelis, commanded by Colonel Moshe Bar-Kochva, fought a bitterly contested armoured battle around Kabatiya that began on 6 June and was to last until the early hours of the following day.

However, this diverted Jordanian attention sufficiently to allow a second Israeli armoured brigade, under Colonel Uri Ram, to skirt Jenin to the east and move onto the road to Tubas and Nablus, behind enemy lines. Ram encountered stiff opposition from dug-in Jordanian infantry but late on 6 June he broke through to capture Nablus, the key to road communications in Samaria. Early the next morning elements of Ben Ari's brigade, advancing north from Ramallah, linked up with Ram and together they exploited eastwards, towards the Jordan River. Jordanian defences in Samaria fell apart. 40th Armoured Brigade, facing encirclement between Nablus and

Kabatiya, tried to fight its way to the Damiya Bridge on 7 June but, pursued by Bar-Kochva, harassed by the IAF and ambushed by units of Ram's and Ben Ari's brigades, the Jordanians finally abandoned their tanks and made their escape on foot.

At 2000 on 7 June Hussein accepted a ceasefire, effectively handing over the whole of the West Bank to the Israelis. His army, having suffered an estimated 6000 casualties and the loss of nearly all its equipment, had ceased to be a viable force. The Israelis, by contrast, had lost 550 killed and about 2500 wounded but had gained, for the first time, an effective measure of territorial depth as well as control of the symbolic city of Jerusalem.

The attack on the Golan Heights

But the war was still not over, for the Syrian threat remained. At first the Israelis were content to accept the lack of a major Syrian assault on eastern Galilee as an unexpected bonus, taking advantage of the obvious failure of Arab cooperation to concentrate forces in Sinai and the West Bank. But as these campaigns drew to a close and the scale of Syrian artillery strikes against border settlements increased, domestic pressure began to grow for a punitive attack to remove the Syrians from the dominating heights of the Golan plateau. By 8 June the Israeli Cabinet, despite fears of heavy casualties and international outcry, had authorised Elazar to prepare for offensive action.

His task was a daunting one. The

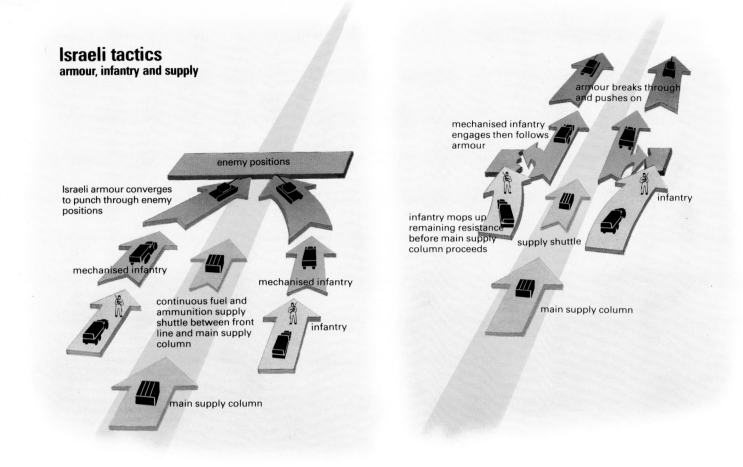

Israeli tactics
armour, infantry and supply

enemy positions

Israeli armour converges to punch through enemy positions

mechanised infantry

continuous fuel and ammunition supply shuttle between front line and main supply column

mechanised infantry

infantry

main supply column

armour breaks through and pushes on

mechanised infantry engages then follows armour

infantry mops up remaining resistance before main supply column proceeds

supply shuttle

infantry

main supply column

western edge of the Golan Heights – the Syrian-Israeli border since 1949 – was a steep escarpment, rising to 760m (2500 ft) in places, the upper levels of which had been extensively fortified by the Syrian Army, under Soviet tutelage. All Israeli movements in eastern Galilee were under constant observation, and fire from an estimated 265 Syrian artillery pieces could be quickly brought to bear. Even if Israeli troops managed to reach the foot of the escarpment intact, they then faced slopes as steep as 1-in-8 over rocky, exposed ground, before encountering the first in a series of in-depth defences – minefields, barbed-wire, dug-in artillery, tanks and concrete blockhouses – which stretched across the plateau almost as far as Damascus.

These positions were permanently manned by three infantry brigades, with T–34s and Su–100s intermixed, and they were supported by a further three infantry, two armoured and two mechanised brigades, normally held back between Kuneitra and Damascus. Elements of these supporting formations had, in fact, been moved forward, concentrating to the west of Kuneitra, on 5/6 June, creating a solid phalanx of military power which further reinforced the defences.

Elazar did enjoy some advantages, however. Since the air strikes of 5 June the Syrian Air Force had lost much of its impact and the IAF, freed from the campaigns in Sinai and the West Bank by the 8th, was available to give almost unlimited fire-support. The same applied to ground forces, for although Northern Command was initially weak, Elazar could expect considerable reinforcement as units redeployed from their areas of victory in the south. Finally, the Israelis enjoyed an element of surprise and this was significantly enhanced when Elazar chose to concentrate his attack in the far north where the escarpment was at its steepest. Working on the presumption that the Syrian defences would be marginally weaker in areas where the terrain seemed impassable, he ordered his chief of staff, Major-General Dan Laner, to launch a two-brigade attack against a series of Syrian positions centred upon Banias. The going would still be extremely hard, but if the attack succeeded the entire Syrian defensive line could be out-flanked and 'rolled up'.

The plan was for the 'Golani' Infantry Brigade, under Colonel Yona Efrat, to advance on the left, aiming towards fortified enemy positions at Tel Azaziat

and Tel Faher before pushing northeastwards to Banias and the foothills of Mount Hermon, at 2750m (9000ft) the dominant feature of the entire Golan area. At the same time an armoured brigade, commanded by Colonel Avraham ('Albert') Mandler, would break through on the right towards Q'ala and Za'ura and the road to Kuneitra. Diversionary attacks further south, around the Benot Ya'akov Bridge, would attract Syrian reserves and, once units began to arrive from Samaria, act as a second avenue of approach to Kuneitra.

Achieving the impossible

The campaign began at 1000 on 9 June under a strong IAF umbrella. The Golani Brigade had the most difficult task, being expected not just to climb the escarpment but also to take the formidable fortifications around Tel Azaziat. A frontal assault would clearly be suicidal, so Efrat ordered his men to infiltrate to the right, aiming for Tel Faher to the east before circling back to attack Tel Azaziat from the rear. Even this was an exceptionally difficult move, made possible only by the bravery and self-sacrifice of the Golani conscripts. Casualties were heavy but, with close IAF support, surprising progress was made. By 1800 on 9 June Tel Faher had been captured after savage hand-to-hand fighting, isolating Tel Azaziat which fell a few hours later. During the night the outer defences of Banias were breached.

Meanwhile Mandler had achieved the impossible. Advancing in single file in full view of Syrian defenders and under a hail of enemy artillery fire, his Shermans crawled up the escarpment behind armoured bulldozers and reached the plateau. Losses were almost crippling – one battalion was reduced to only two tanks by the end of the day – but as Q'ala and Za'ura fell, a significant gap opened up in the Syrian defences, threatening the main Mas'ada–Kuneitra road. To the south infantry units captured high ground around the Benot Ya'akov Bridge, allowing Ram's armoured brigade, hastily redeployed from Samaria, to move eastwards towards Kuneitra, creating a broad arc of Israeli advance which confused and demoralised the enemy.

The capture of Mount Hermon

On 10 June the pressure was maintained. In the north the Golani Brigade was reinforced by Bar-Kochva's redeployed armour and together they took Banias and pushed into the foothills of Mount Hermon (the summit of which was captured by heliborne infantry in the afternoon). They continued into Mas'ada before turning south to link up with Mandler, whose forces had entered Kuneitra without firing a shot at about 1400. Syrian defences had by this time collapsed. Abandoning their positions and much of their equipment, Syrian troops poured eastwards along the road to Damascus, leaving the Israelis in possession of the whole of northern Golan. At much the same time Peled began to clear the southern area, using Gur's paratroops, fresh from their triumphs in Jerusalem, to leap-frog in helicopters from Tawfiq, near the southern tip of the Sea of Galilee, through Fiq, El Al and Butmiyeh to capture the road junction at Rafid. By

1830, with the Syrians in full flight, a ceasefire was imposed. The Israelis, for the loss of 152 killed and 306 wounded, had secured one of the most important strategic features on their borders in a campaign which had lasted less than 30 hours. In addition, the Syrians had been badly mauled, losing about 1000 killed as well as over 100 tanks and most of their front-line artillery.

Thus in three campaigns over a period of only six days the Israelis had defeated their major Arab enemies and significantly improved their strategic position. With Sinai as a buffer against Egyptian attack, the West Bank providing territorial depth to Israel proper and the Golan Heights cleared of Syrian artillery, the potential for security had been created. But it was to be difficult to realise. The Arab powers, humiliated, defeated and deprived of nearly 67,000 sq. km (26,000 sq. miles) of territory, dedicated themselves to recovery and revenge.

Israeli triumph. Opposite: A soldier at the Wailing Wall. Opposite below: Israeli troops pass captured Egyptians. Below: An IDF soldier guarding one of the newly taken Holy Places in Jerusalem. Right: The Israeli territorial gains of 1967. Below right: Egyptian officers under close guard.

The new frontiers
12 June 1967

_ _ _ _ _ Pre 1967 war Israeli frontiers

DAMASCUS • / LEBANON / SYRIA / MEDITERRANEAN / River Jordan / Tel Aviv / Amman • / Jerusalem • / Gaza • / DEAD SEA / Port Said • / El Arish • / ISRAEL / JORDAN / Suez Canal / Suez • / Nakhl • / Elat • / GULF OF SUEZ / SINAI / EGYPT / SAUDI ARABIA / • Sharm El Sheikh / RED SEA

מקום קדוש
הכניסה לזרים אסורה

HOLY PLACE
UNAUTHORISED ENTRY IS FORBIDDEN
BY ORDER

Casualties in 1967

Israeli	Egyptian front	Jordanian front	Syrian front	TOTAL
Killed	275	299	115	689
Wounded	800	1457	306	2563
Arab(estimates)				
Killed	10,000	1000	2500	13,500
Wounded	20,000	2000	5000	27,000

7. Attrition and Terror

The shattering defeat inflicted on them in the Six Day War of June 1967 reverberated throughout the Arab world. Nasser stood before his stunned people and announced his intention to resign, but instead the demand for him to remain as leader was utterly overwhelming from both home and abroad. Nasser survived mainly by virtue of his extraordinary charisma but also because by that time Egypt was controlled by an effective internal security apparatus. This was to become increasingly repressive in Nasser's declining years as the various Opposition parties, from the Marxist left to the radical religious right, gathered their forces. At the same time the Egyptians drew their own conclusions from a resounding military defeat which demonstrated the infeasibility of an extremist position. An Israel with proven military strength and at least the possibility of nuclear weapons could not be obliterated without the destruction of the major Arab cities. Reluctantly and slowly the Egyptians came increasingly to acknowledge what they had known in their hearts for two decades – Israel was to be an enduring reality in the affairs of the Middle East.

This lesson had proved a most costly one for the Jordanians. Jordan is a small country. It does not have the large population of Egypt or even Syria and lacks the military power of Israel. Neither does it possess the natural resources or the wealth of Saudi Arabia or Iraq. In June 1967, though its forces had fought bravely, they had been savagely mauled, some at the time believed beyond the point of recovery. The closure of the Suez Canal as a

Above: Yasser Arafat, the man who welded the Palestinian Liberation Organisation into a formidable force on the world stage, but whose military resources were always small.

result of the war rendered their only port (at Aqaba) virtually useless and the country to all intents and purposes landlocked. The Israeli conquest of the West Bank and Arab Jerusalem had robbed the state of a prime source of revenue from tourism in the Holy Land, and flooded Jordan with more refugees than the administration could handle.

The new Arab unity

Faced with imminent collapse, King Hussein took the initiative and in August 1967 called for a summit conference of

the Arab League powers. Jordan may be small, but her particular involvement in the core issue of Arab politics – the Palestinian problem – produced an immediate and sympathetic response from the leaders who gathered at Khartoum. The summit led to a reconciliation between the radical and conservative elements of the Arab world, manifested in a flow of funds from the oil-rich states into Egypt and Jordan to help finance post-war reconstruction.

Nevertheless, the communiqué issued at Khartoum still maintained a tough and resolute stand against Israel, insisting that there would be 'no peace, no recognition and no negotiation' until the Arab states could act from a 'position of strength'. This clearly implied a reversal of the military verdict of 1967, something which was made more obvious as the Soviet Union intervened to rebuild the Arab armies. By October 1967, for example, Egypt had received arms shipments to replace 80% of her war losses. At the same time, Nasser ensured a maintenance of basic military strength in Egypt by withdrawing his forces from republican support in Yemen. King Feisal of Saudi Arabia followed suit by cutting off aid to the royalists and by 1970 the civil war was resolved in a compromise between the factions. It was a symbol of renewed Arab unity.

But not everyone in the Arab camp was satisfied, for the lack of success in the Six Day War constituted a major disappointment for the Palestinians. They became convinced in its aftermath that the prospect of a reconquest of Palestine by the Arab front-line states was poor

Above: King Feisal of Saudi Arabia, whose enormously rich but conservative state played a key role in the use of the 'oil weapon'. Above right: Moments of tension and horror. West German police cautiously inspect rooms in which Palestinian terrorists held members of the Israeli Olympic squad hostage, during the Munich Olympics of 1972. Below: Trainee Palestinian guerrillas being instructed in the cleaning of weapons. The flow of recruits into Palestinian terrorist organisations bears testimony to the strength of Palestinian feelings over the existence of Israel.

and that the solution to their problem lay increasingly in their own hands. After 1967 the Palestinians turned more and more to guerrilla activity, designed to wear down the resolve of the Israelis and, through terrorism on an international scale, to exert maximum pressure upon the Jews to come to some form of satisfactory settlement. It was a development which revolutionised Palestinian politics and injected a new force into the Arab world.

Arafat and the PLO

Earlier, in 1963, the Arab governments had proposed the creation of a Palestine Liberation Organisation (PLO) to coordinate the activities of the different guerrilla groups. The PLO was formally established in May 1964 when the first Palestine National Council, consisting of some 400 prominent Palestinians, met in the old part of Jerusalem which was then under Jordanian control. The first chairman was Ahmed Shukeiri, but he proved a most uninspired and ill-tempered leader who commanded little respect. Within a couple of years he was replaced by Yasser Arafat.

Details of Arafat's personal life are scanty. He was born in 1929 into a prominent Palestinian family in Jerusalem. He grew up in Gaza where his father, a wealthy merchant, had business interests. Arafat later went to Cairo University where he studied engineering. In the heady days which followed the downfall of Farouk, Arafat espoused the Palestinian cause and joined the Moslem Brotherhood (an extremist political organisation). He saw service as a lieutenant of engineers in the Egyptian Army during the Suez Campaign of 1956 but later found it expedient to leave Egypt when Nasser cracked down on the Moslem Brotherhood. Like so many of his better-educated countrymen, Arafat took his skills to the Gulf and settled in Kuwait where he worked as a civil engineer. There in 1959 he founded Al-Fatah ('Conquest') among the Palestinian community.

By the time he became chairman of the Executive Council of the PLO, Arafat

had the reputation of a dedicated but low-key leader. He is known as *al-Ikhtyar* or 'the old man' to his followers. Some Middle East commentators have since cast him in the role of a 'Tito' or 'Castro' of the Palestinian revolution. In part this is because over the years his power and authority have rested on the assumption that no other leading figure within the movement enjoys anything like his stature and reputation.

The defeat of the conventional armies in the Six Day War pointed to the alternative of a sustained guerrilla campaign. However, from the first, success proved elusive, for Israel was an armed camp which offered little in the way of soft targets. Nevertheless the PLO grew in importance in Arab politics despite the fact that it lacked a secure sanctuary and had very few (approximately 15,000) guerrillas to command and send into the field. The movement looked to Syria for sanctuary while Egypt continued to provide diplomatic support and representation abroad. The guerrillas received much of their training from Algerian instructors and, from a safer distance, Saudi Arabia and the Gulf States provided the funds.

Black September

But the existence of the PLO, representing what was to all intents and purposes a state-in-exile, created a dilemma. Should the Palestinians be considered merely as guests in the countries which offered sanctuary – given succour but little else – or should they be regarded as brother Arabs, with the right to organise themselves as best they could in order to recover their lost lands? It was a problem faced most acutely by Jordan. After the Six Day War some 65% of the population of this small state were Palestinians and by August 1970 it was clear that their presence posed a threat to the stability and very integrity of the country. The crisis broke in early September 1970 when members of the Popular Front for the Liberation of Palestine (PFLP) – an extremist faction of the PLO – instigated a series of plane hijacks which resulted in three airliners being flown to Dawson's Field in northern Jordan, where they were blown up. King Hussein, faced with the humiliating prospect of the PLO using his state as if it were their own, reacted strongly. On 17 September, under pressure from a near-mutinous army, he

authorised an all-out assault on Palestinian urban strongholds in and around the capital Amman. There was fierce fighting and bitter resistance which caused an estimated 4000 deaths, before the PLO were defeated.

The PLO appealed to Arab states for help. Tank battalions of the Syrian-controlled Palestine Liberation Army (PLA) crossed the frontier but their intervention came to nothing. Israel threatened to mobilise and the head of the Syrian Air Force, General Hafez al-Assad (who was to take over the country in a military coup in November 1970), refused to provide air support. He knew that to do so would embroil his pilots in air battles which they could not hope to win. Iraq also offered some assistance and an armoured column manoeuvred just inside the Jordanian border, but made no serious attempt to intervene. The Palestinians. In November 1971 four young had just accepted an American-sponsored truce in the 'War of Attrition' which had been raging along the Suez Canal. The PLO were forced to rely on their own resources and by July 1971 all resistance in Jordan had been overcome. The survivors fled into Lebanon and many of

their families followed to swell the ranks in this last centre of independent PLO activity. The events of 1970 left Jordan isolated within the Arab world and aroused bitter hatred among the Palestinians. In November 1971 four young guerrillas assassinated the Jordanian prime minister, Wasfi Tal, while he was on a visit to Cairo. They claimed to belong to a group sworn to avenge the destruction of the *fedayeen* in Jordan. They called their movement Black September. It was a name which was soon to enter the vocabulary of international terrorism: in September 1972 it was Black Septembrists who kidnapped 11 Israeli athletes at the Munich Olympics, none of whom survived.

In view of this background of continued violence, it is hard to believe that peace efforts between Israel and the Arabs had much chance of success. However, between 1967 and 1973, the Middle East became a focal point of international diplomacy. As early as 22 November 1967, after some months of negotiation in the United Nations, the Security Council accepted Resolution 242, a compromise suggested by the British delegation. Resolution 242 emphasised 'the inadmissability of the acquisition of territory by war' and laid down two basic principles for a just and lasting peace. The first called for Israeli withdrawal 'from territories occupied in the recent conflict'. The second required 'acknowledgement of the sovereignty, territorial integrity and political independence of every state in the area and their right to live in peace within secure and recognised boundaries free from threats or acts of force'. The Resolution also requested the Secretary-General of the UN to send a special representative to the countries concerned, to assist efforts to reach a settlement. The Secretary-General nominated Gunnar Jarring, Swedish ambassador to the USSR.

The War of Attrition

Jarring began his mission in December 1967, and his talks soon revealed the weaknesses of the compromise Resolution. The Israelis regarded it as a basis for negotiation. They insisted on direct negotiation with the Arabs (which would have meant Arab recognition of the state of Israel). They also stressed that the Resolution did not require Israeli withdrawal from all the Arab territories occupied in 1967 (i.e. Sinai, the West Bank and the Golan Heights). The Arab states, by comparison, wished to make Resolution 242 the framework of a peace settlement, requiring only a timetable for mutual approval. They naturally insisted on a complete Israeli withdrawal from their lost lands. In August 1968 Jarring was forced to report the failure of his mission.

Diplomatic action was further hampered in September 1968 when President Nasser began a campaign of harassment across the Suez Canal. Heavy artillery barrages caused casualties among the Israeli Canal garrison and Israel retaliated with commando raids deep inside Egypt. The Egyptians checked their efforts but fighting flared up again in 1969 when Nasser called for a 'War of Attrition'.

He hoped to exploit two fundamental Israeli weaknesses, that the economy could not support a long war and that the Israelis themselves would not accept casualties on the same scale as the Egyptians. Diplomatic efforts therefore had to concentrate on achieving a ceasefire as a prelude to negotiations on a permanent settlement.

In April 1969 America began talks with the Soviet Union, but these stalled when the Arabs temporarily seemed to be gaining the upper hand in the War of Attrition and their position hardened. By October the Egyptian advantage had vanished and they were prepared to reconsider their position. They proposed talks between Jarring and the states involved, without a commitment to face-to-face negotiations. The United States and the Soviet Union prepared a brief to guide Jarring in his talks. However this initiative was still-born, because the Israelis refused to accept anything but direct negotiation.

Early in 1970 Israel increased her pressure on Egypt. Over 8 million kg (8000 tons) of bombs were dropped by the Israeli Air Force (IAF) in the first four months of the year. Egyptian pleas for help were followed by direct Soviet involvement in the air defence of Egypt, which gave the Egyptians confidence to begin offensive action on the east bank of the Canal. In return the Israelis increased their efforts. In order to break the process of escalation, in May the American Secretary of State William Rogers proposed a ceasefire, to be followed by a revival of the Jarring mission, using

Opposite far left: A Palestinian refugee weeps in the wreckage of her home in a camp in the Gaza Strip. Opposite above and below: The Dawson's Field hijacking incident in 1970 culminated in the destruction of the three airliners involved. The inability of the Jordanian government to control PLO activities led directly to the Jordanian Army's attack on Palestinian strongholds in September. Left: Jordanian forces searching for PLO guerrillas near the Syrian border late in September 1970.

Resolution 242 as the starting point for negotiations. Neither side showed any initial enthusiasm for the Rogers Plan and the air war over the Canal increased in intensity. The Soviets and Egyptians pushed their surface-to-air-missile (SAM) bases closer to the Canal and the Israelis struck back at the bases. In July 1970 the Israelis lost seven aircraft without affecting the advance of the SAM bases, although they did shoot down four Soviet-manned aircraft on 30 July. Mrs Golda Meir, the Israeli prime minister, accepted the Rogers Plan on 31 July. The Egyptians, who had had 10,000 casualties since the beginning of the year, were being pressed by the Soviets to accept the Plan. Rogers suggested a 90-day ceasefire from 7 August, with a freeze on military deployments within 50km (31 miles) of the Canal, and this was accepted.

The Israelis were quick to accuse the Egyptians of breaking the ceasefire terms by constructing SAM sites close to the Canal. America was slow to back these charges but by the end of August had to admit they were justified. The new deployments meant that the Egyptians could now cover parts of the east bank of the Canal with their SAMs, an essential preliminary to an attack on Sinai. The Israelis responded by breaking off negotiations under the Rogers Plan. However, neither side wanted to resume hostilities and the ceasefire continued.

The death of Nasser

On 28 September 1970 President Nasser died. His tenure of power had provided one of the longest, most stable and popular governments in the post-1945 Arab world. It can hardly be considered as a successful period, however, for his failures exceeded his achievements. Yet he was never more popular than in the period immediately following his most humiliating defeat in the Six Day War. Nasser was more fortunate than his numerous contemporaries who attempted to govern tempestuous Syria or Iraq. Egypt never possessed the ethnic divisions and internal schisms which thwarted those who sought to rule in Damascus or Baghdad. Egypt was a country which by the time it acquired

Right: The funeral cortège of Nasser, swamped as it moves through crowds of Egyptians. Nasser's death on 28 September 1970 removed one of the leading actors from the drama of Middle East politics. Below right: A march in London in 1970 to commemorate Nasser. Bottom right: Moamar al-Gaddafi (left) and Anwar el-Sadat; in their different ways, each saw himself as Nasser's heir.

complete independence had developed a mature polity and a solid national consciousness.

Nasser's style of leadership perhaps reflects more closely than anything else that his popularity lay with him being very much a man of his time. His ability lay not in the skill to resolve outstanding problems but rather in the fact that he addressed those issues which were always to the forefront of opinion in both Egypt and the Arab world. It was the deep public concern he showed over such diverse issues as industrial and social reform in Egypt, the expulsion of foreign influence and the Palestine problem, rather than their resolution, which made him so popular.

All of these considerations are valid despite the fact that by the time of his death, Nasser had taken Egypt militarily into the Soviet fold. There were about 20,000 Soviet military personnel in the country, ostensibly to train the Egyptians and protect them from the Israelis. Their outrageously racist behaviour, together with their total lack of sympathy for local custom and tradition, made their presence increasingly resented. In some senses the only bright spot on the horizon for Nasser in his declining years was the military coup in neighbouring Libya and the emergence of another convert to the radicalist Arab camp.

Libya, liberated from the Italians and administered by the British after 1943, was first formed into an independent kingdom on 1 January 1952 under Idris, King of the Senussi. For many years the new state drew its revenues in the form of rents that the British and, to a much greater extent, the Americans, paid for their extensive military bases. Such overt dependence on the West earned the scorn of Nasser and the radical Arabs. The

discovery of oil in Libya made the military rents of no consequence but did little to improve the quality of a corrupt and incompetent regime. In 1969 Colonel Moamar al-Gaddafi's military coup ushered in the new era.

No leader since Nasser has had so much charisma for the Arab masses as Gaddafi, his most devoted disciple. Much to the discomfort and frequent embarrassment of the Arab world, Gaddafi has sought to don the mantle of the leader and is dedicated to spreading his own gospel, an eccentric mix of Islam and socialism. Convinced of his own genius, Gaddafi dreams of an Islamic sub-Saharan Republic which would extend from Senegal to the Sudanese Republic. From the first, he found little support from Nasser's Egypt and even less under the new president, Anwar el-Sadat.

Sadat and the Soviets

When Nasser died, Sadat was not expected to last long in power. Although he surprised observers by purging his main rivals from the government in May 1971 he was under constant domestic pressure to improve Egypt's position against Israel. He declared 1971 the 'Year of Decision' but his credit was weakened by the lack of action. By 1972 Sadat was losing his patience with diplomatic efforts and tiring of the Soviet Union as a partner. He suspected that the Soviets were more interested in maintaining their new relationship of détente with the United States than in settling the Middle Eastern problem. The communiqué issued after the Nixon–Brezhnev summit in Moscow in May 1972 convinced the Arabs that the superpowers were determined to leave the Middle East in cold storage.

Sadat's first move was to expel the Soviet military advisers in July 1972. By this move, he freed the Egyptian military from Soviet supervision and improved his standing at home and in the Arab world. He did not break completely with Moscow, however, and in October, with Syrian mediation, he arranged for Soviet arms deliveries to begin again on an unprecedented scale. An even larger deal followed in February 1973. For in November 1972 Sadat had decided to use

military means against Israel, in a joint attack with President Assad's Syria. A 'United Command Structure' was established in January 1973.

Even with their new Soviet weapons the Egyptian and Syrian generals did not believe that they could destroy Israel. Instead, their aim was to change the existing balance of Middle Eastern affairs by undermining the basic assumptions of Israeli defence policy. The chosen method was a limited offensive to demonstrate that Israel's borders could not be guaranteed and that the power of her air force and armoured corps was not unlimited. We know something about the details of Egyptian planning, whereas the Syrians have revealed little of the thinking behind their plan.

Below: The SA-7, a portable, cheap Soviet anti-aircraft missile bought by the Egyptians. The relative effectiveness of such weapons would, it was hoped, end the Israeli dominance in mobile warfare that had proved so devastating in 1967.

Shazli's plans

The driving force behind the Egyptian plan was General Saad el Din Shazli, chief of staff from May 1971 (and erstwhile commander of Shazli Force in Sinai in 1967). Shazli's plan combined an offensive strategy with defensive tactics; according to von Moltke the strongest form of war. The Egyptians faced three major problems: the IAF, the Canal barrier itself and the expected Israeli armoured counter-attacks. Shazli's solution to the first problem was to restrict his offensive to a zone 10–13km (6–8 miles) east of the Canal, which could be covered by SAMs from the west bank of the Canal. The Egyptian Air Force was not to tackle the IAF, but restrict itself to ground strikes where Israeli defences were weakest.

After detailed studies of the Canal, Egyptian engineers developed special techniques for breaching the 25m (82ft) high embankment, using high-pressure pumps to wash away 1500 cu. m (1962

cu. yd) of sand to make each gap. Soviet pontoon bridges and amphibious ferries were acquired to enable vehicles to cross the 200m (220yd) wide Canal. Steps were also taken to neutralise a system which the Egyptians believed the Israelis operated for flooding the Canal with burning napalm. To deal with the Israeli armoured threat the leading waves of infantry were provided with portable antitank weapons, ranging from the RPG–7 shoulder-fired rocket and re-coilless rifles to the Sagger wire-guided missile. The rest of the army was stripped of its antitank weapons to thicken the screen in Sinai to the utmost. Shazli also decided to attack on the broadest possible front, so that the Israelis would

The assault on the Bar–Lev line over the Suez Canal required careful preparation. Above: One of the pontoon bridges erected by Egyptian engineers to move the necessary supplies across. Right: The Soviet-built GSP amphibious vehicles used to ferry tanks and heavy equipment. Below: Communicating by field telephone and ferrying supplies across the Canal.

Above: Saad el Din Shazli. As Egyptian chief of staff from 1971, Shazli master-minded the Egyptian attacks across the Suez Canal in 1973. Right: Israeli developments in weaponry went on apace in the 1970s. Here an L-33, a self-propelled gun based on a Sherman chassis but with a 155mm M68 gun-howitzer, goes on parade.

be unable to concentrate their forces without leaving the Egyptians safely consolidating their hold on most of the front.

Egyptian staff work was meticulously detailed, down to the provision of the smallest item of equipment, such as new water bottles for the infantry. Over 2000 carts were supplied to enable the leading infantry to carry forward the vast quantities of ammunition they would need for the first battles, before the Canal bridges were operating. Great emphasis was placed on training the individual soldier, with frequent rehearsals of his allotted task. Fortunately for the Egyptians, at El Ballah, south of Qantara, the Canal splits into two channels, one of which was completely in Egyptian territory and provided an ideal training ground.

The Syrian complication

The alliance with Syria complicated Shazli's plans. General Ahmed Ismail, the Minister of War, knew that the Syrians would expect more than just a limited attack if they were to risk a war with Israel. He therefore ordered Shazli to prepare plans for an advance towards the crucial Passes which control movement in Sinai – the Khatmia, Giddi and Mitla. Shazli violently opposed this because he did not want to risk his forces in the sort of open, mobile battle at which the Israelis excelled. But Ismail insisted on having a plan to show the Syrians, although he agreed that it would only be used in the event of overwhelming success in the first phase of the war. Shazli condemned this 'political' interference, but it could be justified militarily because the Syrian attack would tie down Israeli reserves in the north which would otherwise deploy to Sinai.

Final conferences between the Egyptian and Syrian staffs led to the choice of 6 October for the attack. Tidal conditions in the Canal were most suitable then, the weather would be favourable in Sinai and the Golan, and a long, dark night would cover the Canal crossings. In addition it would be Yom Kippur ('The Day of Atonement'), when Israeli transport and communications systems would be halted. The operation was code-named 'Badr' because it would begin on the tenth day of Ramadan, the anniversary of Mohammed's first victory at the battle of Badr. Each army wanted to attack with the sun behind it, at dawn for the Syrians and at dusk for the Egyptians. They compromised on 1400 hours.

Israeli intelligence

Since 1973 a great deal has been made of the Israeli failure to anticipate the Arab attack. There was no lack of warning. Israeli intelligence had a good picture of Egyptian and Syrian mobilisations and deployments towards the border. They knew the Egyptian plan in outline, although not the timings. All the evidence was available to trigger an Israeli alert in time to mobilise reserves before the attack began. However the correct conclusions were not drawn. Egyptian troop movements were explained in terms of the exercises which happened every autumn. The Syrian measures were seen as a response to an air battle in September and

Israel recycled the Sherman chassis in many forms: as the M50 SPG (above) and the Soltam 160mm mortar (right).

The War of Attrition

The 'War of Attrition' was the name given by President Nasser to the strategy by which he hoped to recover from the losses of the Six Day War. The Egyptians knew that the Israelis excelled in short, mobile wars but believed that an extended, static, slogging match would be to the Egyptian advantage. The Israelis were very sensitive to casualties whereas the Egyptians had large reserves of manpower. The strategy was therefore to cause the Israelis casualties by artillery bombardments, air attacks and commando raids across the Suez Canal, until public opinion demanded peace negotiations. Success in such operations would also help to restore Egypt's battered morale and perhaps reassert Egypt's role as the main 'front-line' state.

The plan was tried out in September and October 1968 and the Israelis lost nearly 50 casualties. Out-gunned along the Canal, they replied by using heliborne commandos to raid targets in the Nile Valley. The Egyptians ceased operations while they reorganised their defences.

The War of Attrition proper began in March 1969. During the lull the Israelis had built the Bar-Lev line so their Canal garrison did not suffer as heavily as the Egyptians had hoped, but the artillery assault was supplemented by a very active programme of commando raids into Sinai. In July one such raiding party caused 11 casualties in an Israeli tank laager south of Port Tewfik.

The Egyptians deployed over 1000 guns along the Canal, including many of the latest Soviet weapons. The Israeli artillery was inferior in both numbers and quality, although they had some successes, such as the lucky shot which killed the Egyptian chief of staff, General Riadh, in March 1969. Unable to match the Egyptians along the Canal, the Israelis returned to their 'indirect approach', launching commando raids into Egypt. One of the most effective was the attack on Green Island, a fortress protecting Suez, on 19 July.

However the commando raids did not stop the Egyptian shelling so the Israeli Air Force was called in to redress the balance. The Egyptian Air Force tried to protect their ground forces and dogfights over the Canal were common. In the first two months 21 Egyptian aircraft were lost, against three Israeli. The numbers of the Israelis were also able to overwhelm the Egyptian surface-to-air missile defences, based on the SAM-2 missile.

Two daring Israeli ground raids should be mentioned. On 9 September 1969 they landed in captured Egyptian tanks and APCs on the Egyptian side of the Gulf of Suez and rampaged about 50km (31 miles) before re-embarking with little loss. On 27 December they snatched one of the latest Soviet radars from the installation at Ras Gharib.

In January 1970 the Israelis launched a series of air raids against targets deep inside Egypt, in order to show the Egyptian public that its government's success claims were unfounded. In his concern at this development Nasser appealed for more Soviet help and received it. Thousands of Soviet personnel arrived to set up a new air-defence system, combining Soviet-manned SAM sites and aircraft. The Israelis ended their deep raids but the war over the Canal continued. The Soviet presence in their rear allowed the Egyptians to devote more aircraft to the Canal war. In March, April and May, the Israelis lost over 200 casualties. They replied with heavier and heavier air raids; for example, in just one week of June 1970 they dropped 4000 bombs along the Canal. The climax of this period came on 30 July when the Israelis shot down four Soviet aircraft.

This incident also marked the end of the War of Attrition. Both sides realised that they were stalemated. Nothing was being achieved by the fighting, and as its intensity escalated, the danger of superpower intervention increased. Both sides therefore accepted the ceasefire proposed by the US Secretary of State, William Rogers.

Above: Patrolling the Golan Heights.

to fears of an Israeli attack. A skilful Arab deception plan increased this false sense of security. Obvious defensive preparations were made on both fronts and other measures included Egyptian demobilisation of 20,000 men and the announcement that army officers could apply to go on pilgrimage.

However the basic reason for Israeli unpreparedness lay in the over-confidence which resulted from the apparent ease of victory in 1967. This had led to what was called 'The Concept' – a firm and oft-repeated belief that Egypt would not begin a major war until she could be sure of defeating the IAF and that Syria would never attack Israel except in co-operation with Egypt. Because the Egyptian Air Force was still relatively weak in 1973, the Israelis were easily convinced that an attack was impossible. Indeed, when a junior intelligence officer in Sinai concluded that the Egyptians were about to attack, having rightly seen through their deception measures, his superior suppressed his report because it did not accord with 'The Concept'. At root the IDF was so arrogantly sure of its superiority in every department that no-one could conceive of the Arabs daring to attack. In particular the Israelis did not see that even a very limited military success was a very tempting prospect to the Arabs.

The consequence was that as late as 5 October the chances of a war were assessed as 'the lowest of the low' and only very limited alert measures were initiated over the Yom Kippur holiday. At 0400 on 6 October the Israelis learnt of the coming attack, but understood that it would begin at 1800 hours. They were totally surprised by the bombardment when it began at 1400.

8. Yom Kippur

There were five Egyptian infantry divisions in line along the Suez Canal on 6 October 1973, each reinforced by a tank brigade. From the Mediterranean to the Bitter Lakes was the Second Army sector, with, from north to south, the 18th, 2nd and 16th Infantry Divisions. South of the Lakes was Third Army with the 7th and 19th Infantry Divisions. Each Army had an armoured and a mechanised division in its second echelon. The plan called for each division to establish a bridgehead approximately 7km (4 miles) wide and 3km (2 miles) deep within the first three or four hours. By this time most of the divisions' infantry battalions and their immediate support would be in Sinai and the first bridges and ferries should be ready. In the second phase during the night, the divisions' tanks and artillery were to cross and by dawn the divisional bridgeheads were to be linked up into two army bridgeheads and any Israeli positions still holding out were to be eliminated. The army bridgeheads were to run along the 'Artillery Road', 10km (6 miles) inside Sinai, which had been built to allow the Israeli self-propelled guns to redeploy quickly from sector to sector. Although plans existed for a breakout from the bridgeheads towards the Sinai Passes, the Egyptian High Command intended to introduce an 'operational pause' before these were implemented and hoped to draw the Israelis into a battle of attrition fought from prepared Egyptian defences under the cover of the SAM batteries on the west bank.

The Egyptians attack

The Egyptian plan was precisely timed. At 1355 hours on 6 October 240 aircraft crossed the Canal to attack Israeli airfields, Hawk SAM bases, command posts, long-range artillery and administrative centres in Sinai. This was the signal for the 2000 guns of the Egyptian artillery to begin nearly an hour's bombardment of the east bank. In the first minute alone 10,500 shells rained down – 175 shells a second. Because the Israeli garrison, strung out in strongpoints known as the 'Bar-Lev line', was so small (only 436 men) and deployed inside concrete bunkers, their casualties were quite low, but the barrage did ensure that the defenders could do little to oppose the Egyptian crossing. At 1415 8000 infantry began to paddle across the Canal in rubber assault boats. They were supported by tanks and field-guns in prepared positions on top of the western embankment firing directly at the Israeli forts. Generally the infantry tried to bypass the Israeli strongpoints and pushed on to establish a defensive perimeter in the desert. Antitank teams prepared ambushes and laid mines in the path of the expected Israeli armoured counter-attack. Behind these screens engineers began to breach the Canal bank and prepare crossing sites.

The Egyptians had correctly anticipated the Israeli counter-attack plan, code-named *Shovach Yonim* ('Pigeon Left'). The Sinai garrison consisted of a

Israel 1973

Pre 1967 war Israeli frontiers

Damascus ●
SYRIA
LEBANON
River Jordan
MEDITERRANEAN
Tel Aviv ●
Amman ●
Jerusalem ●
● Gaza
DEAD SEA
● Port Said
El Arish ●
ISRAEL
JORDAN
Suez Canal
● Suez
Nakhl ●
● Elat
GULF OF SUEZ
SINAI
EGYPT
SAUDI ARABIA
● Sharm El Sheikh
RED SEA

Comparative forces 1973			
Israel	men/army 275,000	tanks 1700	aircraft 432
Egypt	285,000	2000	600
Syria	100,000	1200	210

Left: Israel's frontiers in 1973, the situation that had existed since 1967 and that the Egyptians and Syrians hoped to change utterly. Above: The relative strengths of the combatants in 1973. Opposite above: The Egyptian attack across the Canal that took the defenders of the Bar-Lev line by surprise and set the Israelis a new set of problems to solve.

reserve infantry brigade holding the Bar-Lev line and three regular armoured brigades, under the command of Major-General Shmuel Gonen. Gonen was renowned in the army as a very courageous but harsh tank commander, feared rather than loved by his subordinates. The armoured brigades were under the command of Major-General Avraham ('Albert') Mandler's divisional headquarters, and two other armoured divisions were allocated to reach Sinai in the early stages of mobilisation. Both were reserve divisions. One was commanded by Major-General Avraham ('Bren') Adan, commander of the Israeli armoured corps, and the other by the recently retired General Ariel ('Arik') Sharon.

Both generals were well acquainted with Sinai. Adan had planned the Bar-Lev fortifications and Sharon had only handed over the Sinai command to Gonen in the previous July. But however experienced, the Israeli commanders

The Bar-Lev Line

The Bar-Lev line was built as rapidly as possible during a lull in the cross-Canal fighting in the winter of 1968-69. Twenty-six *moazim* or strongpoints were built, at intervals of about 10km (7 miles) along the Canal. Each was designed for a garrison of 18 to 30 men. A typical *moaz* consisted of four fighting positions, each with its own bunker, connected to a central bunker which provided a command post, living accommodation and a medical post. The bunkers were constructed of concrete, reinforced with rails from the disused Sinai railway and covered with sand, kept in place by steel mesh. The positions were surrounded by a trench, a sand embankment, barbed wire fences and mines. The garrison had normal infantry weapons, with nothing larger than a heavy machine-gun.

The chain of observation posts was backed by a considerable infrastructure. Two roads were built running north–south parallel to the Canal at distances of 10km and 30km (7 and 20 miles) to the east of it. The first, known as the Artillery Road, enabled self-propelled artillery

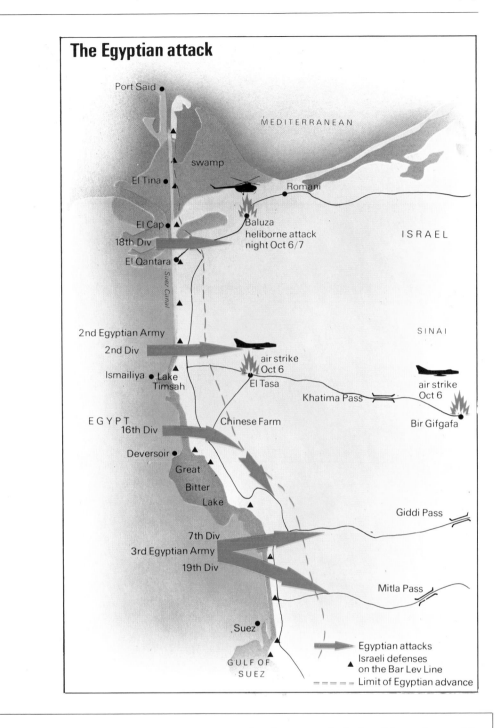

The Egyptian attack

Port Said

MEDITERRANEAN

swamp

El Tina

Romani

El Cap

Baluza
heliborne attack
night Oct 6/7

ISRAEL

18th Div

El Qantara

Suez Canal

2nd Egyptian Army

2nd Div

air strike
Oct 6

SINAI

Ismailiya • Lake
Timsah

El Tasa

air strike
Oct 6

Khatima Pass

EGYPT

Chinese Farm

Bir Gifgafa

16th Div

Deversoir

Great
Bitter
Lake

Giddi Pass

7th Div

3rd Egyptian Army

19th Div

Mitla Pass

Suez

Egyptian attacks
Israeli defenses
on the Bar Lev Line
Limit of Egyptian advance

GULF OF
SUEZ

batteries to move rapidly between their fire positions. The first line of armoured reserves was also held here, ready to dash forward to firing ramps set in the strongpoints and the Canal bank between them. The second road permitted the main armoured reserves and logistic units to concentrate for a major counter-attack. East–west roads linked the lateral roads with the Canal. A comprehensive network of buried cables provided secure communications for the line, backed by several radio nets. The line was com-

pleted two weeks before Nasser began his War of Attrition in March 1969 and served its purpose well in that conflict.

The Bar-Lev line provides a classic example of the psychological dangers of relying on a system of fortifications. Built to provide security for observation posts and early warning of an attack, the line was described in the Israeli and foreign press as if it were another Maginot line, designed to fight a major battle. Even the Israeli Army, which should have known better, seems to have believed the myth.

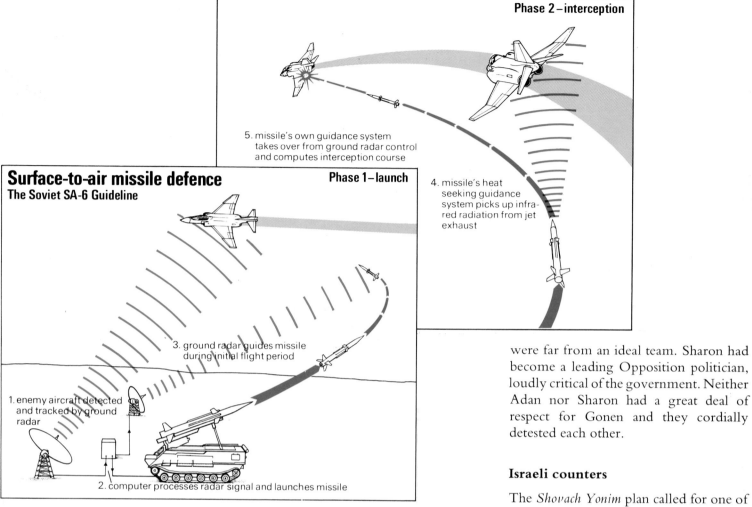

Surface-to-air missile defence
The Soviet SA-6 Guideline

Phase 2 – interception

5. missile's own guidance system takes over from ground radar control and computes interception course

4. missile's heat seeking guidance system picks up infra-red radiation from jet exhaust

Phase 1 – launch

3. ground radar guides missile during initial flight period

1. enemy aircraft detected and tracked by ground radar

2. computer processes radar signal and launches missile

Top: How the SA-6 missiles proved so dangerous to Israeli fighters. Above: An SA-2 'Guideline'. Opposite left: A Soviet-built missile radar station, part of the Egyptian anti-aircraft screen. Opposite right: The Egyptian flag flies over the Bar-Lev line.

were far from an ideal team. Sharon had become a leading Opposition politician, loudly critical of the government. Neither Adan nor Sharon had a great deal of respect for Gonen and they cordially detested each other.

Israeli counters

The *Shovach Yonim* plan called for one of Mandler's brigades to deploy into the Bar-Lev line, covering the gaps between individual forts with platoons of tanks. The other two brigades were to be used as immediate counter-attack forces. The plan assumed at least 48 hours' warning time, which would have allowed the reserve divisions to reach Sinai, where they would have been used against any major Egyptian lodgement on the east bank. Preparations had also been made to take the battle into Egypt with an early crossing of the Canal. A strength of the Israeli Army is that it gives the widest possible initiative to commanders, but a complementary weakness is that this can lead to endless arguments and confusion. This is what happened to *Shovach Yonim*.

Mandler was unwilling to send tanks to the Bar-Lev line before the war started, lest they be caught by the Egyptian barrage. He therefore delayed the order until after midday which meant that the Bar-Lev line gaps were left uncovered and the advancing Israeli tanks were

ambushed by the first wave of Egyptian infantry and suffered heavily. So basic a change in the plan should have been made before the war started.

The success of the Egyptian plan exceeded their generals' hopes. They were prepared for 30,000 casualties, a third of them killed during the crossing, but the first phase was completed with only 208 Egyptian dead. However the Egyptians were not equally successful everywhere. An independent brigade which was sent across the northernmost part of the Canal, into the marshes along the Mediterranean coast, was quickly repulsed. This was not serious because it was probably intended primarily as a diversion. The Second Army reached its objectives on time, although some Israeli outposts still held out. In the south, Third Army ran into difficulties when it was discovered that the Canal bank, being made of clay, could not be washed away by the high-pressure hoses, as could the sandy bank of the north. The clay turned to mud, and the exits from the bridges were soon quagmires. Third Army's infantry completed their crossing, but their heavy support was delayed until bulldozers could be brought up and used to make new gaps.

Swimming the Bitter Lake

The Egyptians had also planned to launch heliborne commandos into Sinai to attack HQs and seize the exits from the Mitla and Giddi Passes. Some of these

parties did succeed in adding to the confusion on the Israeli side in the first night, but the main parties were destroyed before they reached the Passes. A Marine Brigade which 'swam' the Bitter Lakes in amphibious tanks and personnel carriers to try to link up with the commandos on 6 October, had the misfortune to meet Mandler's southern forces advancing towards the Canal. The thinly armoured and under-gunned PT-76 amphibious tanks were no match for the Israeli main battle tanks and were annihilated. The Israelis pressed on and were soon adding to the problems on Third Army's front. However the Israelis had only a weak brigade which could not afford the losses it suffered from the salvoes of Egyptian antitank weapons. By dawn on 7 October the surviving tanks were forced to withdraw to refuel and take on ammunition. The Israelis had no reserves and the pressure on Third Army relaxed.

In the north Israeli losses were even greater. When Mandler reported his tank state to Gonen at 0356 on 7 October he had only 110 operational tanks out of the 277 with which he had begun the war. For the rest of that day he tried to contain the Egyptian advance to the Artillery Road.

Meanwhile the Israeli reserve divisions were being pushed forward as quickly as possible, completing their combat grouping as they moved. The restricted Sinai roads were soon choked and the tanks

were ordered to advance on their own tracks off the roads. Gonen was determined to counter-attack as soon as the tanks reached the forward area, even though they would lack infantry and artillery support; he was already talking of crossing the Canal. During the night of 7/8 October a conference of Gonen, his divisional commanders and the Army chief of staff, General David Elazar, agreed on a limited counter-attack which was not to approach the Canal unless there was a general collapse among the Egyptians. Adan's division was to strike southwards from a position level with Kantara. If it was successful, Sharon's division would attack Third Army by moving south from the strategic Tasa crossroads. If Adan's attack failed, Sharon would be equally well placed to reinforce him by swinging north from Tasa.

Gonen repulsed

Gonen's HQ had a wildly over-optimistic picture of the situation along the Canal and during the night Gonen gave orders for a more extensive attack, including attempts to capture Egyptian bridges and reach the west bank. These orders were not received by the divisions before the attack began, which ensured that Gonen and his commanders were completely at cross-purposes in their radio conversations.

At first on 8 October Adan's division seemed to be progressing well, with little Egyptian opposition. However this was because, instead of using the Artillery Road as their axis, his leading brigades had swung south too early and, rather than rolling up the Egyptians from the flank, were moving across the enemy front and exposing their own flank. Turning west to rectify this committed them to a frontal attack. Poor tactical handling by subordinate commanders made matters worse. Thus Colonel Asaf Yaguri's battalion aimed for a surviving Israeli strongpoint at El-Firdan and, ignoring the disappearance of its reconnaissance element, rushed into the 'sack' of a classic antitank ambush, under fire from three sides. Most of the battalion was destroyed in the killing-ground and Yaguri was captured and exhibited, still dazed, on

Egyptian television that evening. Israeli radio nets broke down under Egyptian jamming and interference by Gonen's HQ, desperate to find out what was happening. Adan could not obtain air support because the IAF was committed against Syria. Sharon jumped the gun with his attack, so his forces, having started south, had to be recalled and took no effective part in the day's fighting. Adan's attack was abandoned at 1400 and during the early evening he did manage to check a counter-attack by the tank and mechanised brigades of two Egyptian divisions.

From the night of 8 October the Israelis were generally content to survive on the defensive, making limited thrusts to cover the withdrawal of surviving Bar-Lev garrisons. Sharon did attempt a larger attack, against Gonen's orders, which led Gonen to request Sharon's dismissal. In this atmosphere of recrimination and crisis, the only Israeli gain was that they had discovered a weak spot in the Egyptian line, at the northern end of the Great Bitter Lake.

The Arab offensive in Golan

The Syrian attack on Israel was concentrated in the Golan Plateau, lying between

Above: A Mig-17, the principal close-support fighter of the Egyptian Air Force, in action in Sinai. Right: The Egyptian anti-aircraft screen that gave the ground troops much greater protection than they had known in 1967. Opposite top: A constant problem for the Syrians during the Golan fighting was that Israeli Centurions presented a much smaller target to opponents when in a firing position than did the T-55s and T-62s with which the Arab forces were equipped. Opposite centre: An Israeli lookout on Golan with a 0.3 inch Browning machine-gun. Opposite bottom: The Syrian assaults.

The Egyptian anti-aircraft screen

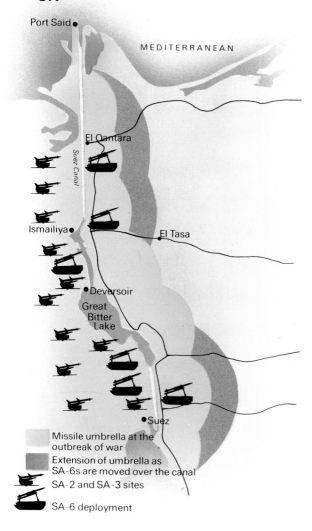

Missile umbrella at the outbreak of war

Extension of umbrella as SA-6s are moved over the canal

SA-2 and SA-3 sites

SA-6 deployment

the Lebanese border at Mount Hermon in the north, and the Sea of Galilee in the south, a front of about 55km (35 miles). The Israelis had captured the plateau in 1967 and since then had developed a strong position along the ceasefire line. The Golan is littered with volcanic mounds and the Israelis had built fortified observation posts on 14 of these close to the border, each held by a platoon of infantry and a platoon of tanks. They had dug a 5m (16ft) deep antitank ditch along most of the line, with other obstacles and minefields laid so as to canalise an advance from the east into killing grounds. Around these, ramps had been built to give tanks the longest possible fields of fire. Limited alert measures had brought the garrison strength up to a brigade of infantry and two armoured brigades, with a total of 177 tanks, by 6 October. In addition, the Israelis had constructed an observation post in the north of their line, on a spur of Mount Hermon, which was packed with sophisticated monitoring equipment and gave them a superb view of the whole plateau.

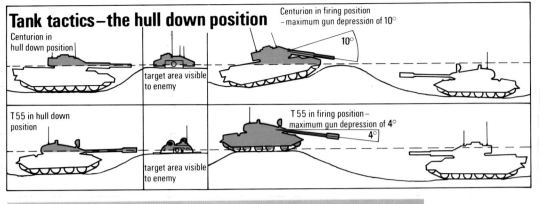

Tank tactics – the hull down position

Centurion in hull down position

Centurion in firing position – maximum gun depression of 10° 10°

target area visible to enemy

T 55 in hull down position

T 55 in firing position – maximum gun depression of 4° 4°

target area visible to enemy

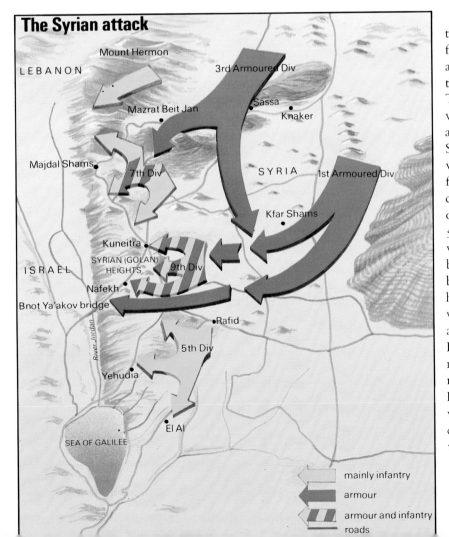

The Syrian attack

Mount Hermon

LEBANON

3rd Armoured Div

Mazrat Beit Jan

Sassa

Knaker

Majdal Shams

7th Div

SYRIA

1st Armoured Div

Kfar Shams

Kuneitra

SYRIAN (GOLAN) HEIGHTS

9th Div

ISRAEL

Nafekh

Bnot Ya'akov bridge

River Jordan

Rafid

5th Div

Yehudia

El Al

SEA OF GALILEE

mainly infantry

armour

armour and infantry

roads

The Syrians had massively re-equipped their army since 1967, changing from a force predominantly of infantry to an armoured and mechanised one. Besides the latest Soviet weapons, such as the T–62 tank, the BMP infantry combat vehicle and the SA–6 mobile surface-to-air missile, they had absorbed much of the Soviet Army's doctrine. Their forces were divided into two echelons. In the first were three mechanised divisions, deployed along the border – the 7th north of Kuneitra, the 9th in the centre and the 5th south of Rafid. These divisions, each with about 200 tanks and in all supported by over 1000 artillery pieces, were to breach the Israeli . defences, punching holes through which the second echelon was to pass. This consisted of two armoured divisions – the 3rd north of Kuneitra and the 1st to the south – whose mission was to push across the Golan and reach the bridges over the River Jordan. However, Soviet operational doctrine was developed in the open steppes, a far cry from the Golan, where only tracked vehicles could move off the few roads, and then only with great difficulty. (After the war the plateau was littered with tracks shed by the tanks of both sides.) On their very constricted axes, the Syrians were unable to exploit the full weight of their armoured masses, and they might have been better advised to develop their own tactics, making more flexible use of ordinary infantry to prise the Israelis out of their positions. In a tank battle on the Golan the defender was bound to have an overwhelming advantage. The Syrians might have benefited, however, from another characteristic Soviet ploy, that of using airborne forces ahead of the armoured thrusts. The Syrians considered trying to seize the crucial Benot Ya'akov Brigade, but never implemented the plan, leaving the Israelis free to rush reinforcements into the southern Golan.

The Syrian attack, coordinated with the Egyptians, began at 1400 on 6 October. For an hour their artillery rained over 1·5 million kg (1500 tons) of explosive onto the Israeli positions. Then their columns advanced, led by mine-clearing and bulldozer tanks and tank-mounted bridges. They suffered at Israeli hands but could not be stopped from breaching the antitank ditch in several places. On Mount Hermon a parachute battalion was landed by helicopter and overran the Israeli observation post. Otherwise the Syrians did not try to capture the Israeli strongpoints, all but three of which held out to the end of the war. The Syrians pushed on as night fell and during the

darkness their front line advanced about 8km (5 miles) to the west. The armoured divisions moved up, ready to boost the attack in daylight.

General Rafael ('Raful') Eitan, the Israeli commander in the Golan, had moved his two armoured brigades into their pre-reconnoitred positions as the Syrian bombardment started. They only just reached them in time. North of Kuneitra was the 7th Armoured Brigade, the élite brigade of the Israeli armoured corps under Colonel Avigdor ('Yanush') Ben-Gal. In the southern sector stood the 188th (Barak) Brigade under Colonel Yitzhak Ben-Shoham, which was considerably weaker in tanks. The 188th Brigade fought a desperate battle against the bulk of two Syrian divisions. Tiny, improvised sub-units held much stronger forces at bay, but next morning, as the Syrian 1st Armoured Division came into the battle, the brigade was crushed. By midday on 7 October 90% of its officers were casualties, including Ben-Shoham and his deputy. Most of southern Golan was in Syrian hands, including Eitan's HQ at Nafekh Camp.

An hour before nightfall one Syrian tank battalion reached the edge of the plateau, only ten minutes' drive from the Benot Ya'akov Bridge. But the Syrians did not push on to complete their victory, for reasons which are not clear. It may be that they were working to a system of precisely timed phases, or perhaps they were trying to keep all their forces in line and were halted by their lack of progress

in the north. Whatever the reason, the moment passed and with it the Syrian chance of victory.

The front stabilises

Israeli reinforcements were pouring into the area. General Dan Laner's reserve division, previously earmarked for the Golan, entered north of the Sea of Galilee, one brigade clearing the route to Nafekh, another advancing through Yehudia. The seriousness of the situation in Golan led the Israeli High Command to divert there another division, under General Moshe ('Musa') Peled, which was intended for Sinai. Peled moved up from the south, along the eastern shore of Galilee, heading for El Al and Rafid. The IAF was also thrown into the battle, in order to hold the breach until the armoured divisions arrived. This meant accepting heavy casualties in order to provide close air support in the face of Syria's intact missile defences, but the desperate situation justified the risk.

On Monday 8 October, Laner's and Peled's forces began to make their presence felt and on 9 October the two Israeli pincers were closing on Rafid, trapping the main body of the Syrian 1st Armoured Division around Hushniya. On the 10th Laner's forces eliminated the Syrians in the Hushniya pocket, breaking into their gun lines and supply dumps, while Peled blocked the Syrian retreat.

Events north of Kuneitra had been equally dramatic. Ben-Gal's front was

naturally divided by the Hermonit feature – a fortified hill to the south-east of Mas'ada. His 1st Battalion was deployed to block the valley between Hermonit and Mas'ada. Another battalion, under Lieutenant-Colonel Avigdor Kahalani, covered the valley. It was after dark on 6 October when the Syrians came within range of the 7th Brigade. The Syrians were better equipped for night-fighting, having infra-red devices for drivers and gunners, whereas Israeli tanks had them only for their drivers. A close-range battle followed from 2200 to 0300. The Syrians made little use of infantry and their armoured advance was checked. The

1st Battalion killed 40 tanks and Kahalani's destroyed another 30. Another Israeli force smashed a Syrian column which tried to outflank the Israeli position to the south through Kuneitra. At 0800 on 7 October the Syrians came on again, a mechanised brigade north of Hermonit and a tank brigade to the south, moving through the burning casualties of the night's fighting. This attack was also foiled and in the afternoon a battalion push south of Kuneitra was annihilated.

The Syrian offensive began again at 2200 hours on 7 October, when the 3rd Armoured Division joined in. This time infantry tank-hunting parties with

Above: A Centurion opens up on Syrian positions near Yehudia, as part of the southern sector of the Israeli defences. Below: 130mm artillery adds its support to the Israeli front line. Opposite: A brief moment of relaxation for the crew of an M109 self-propelled gun during a lull in the action on Golan. The empty ammunition cases are an indication of the intensity of the fighting.

RPG-7s were with the advance. The 7th Brigade had scarcely 40 tanks against probably 500 on the Syrian side. Again it was the Syrians who ran out of steam first, breaking off the attack about 0100 on the 8th. At dawn the Syrians advanced again and the hard-pressed Israeli tank crews began to lose track of the number of individual attacks. The day and night saw a continuous series of artillery barrages, tank attacks and brief pauses to fill the empty shell-racks.

The offensive resumes

The morning of Tuesday 9 October brought another massive attack, concentrated against Kahalani's central sector. With air and artillery support, the Syrians flowed into the gaps between the remnants of the Israeli line. The two sides were intermingled and enemy fire could come from any point of the compass. The Israelis could not withdraw to re-supply and some tanks were soon down to their last couple of shells. Only seven tanks remained in action in the entire brigade. The psychological pressures on soldiers who had been fighting without

proper sleep for four nights and three days should have been enough to break them. But the Syrians were equally exhausted and when a tiny group of the 188th (Barak) Brigade arrived on the scene, the tide finally began to turn in favour of the Israelis. The survivors of the two Syrian divisions were forced back across the antitank ditch.

Two Syrian divisions had been wiped out by the 7th Brigade. In the killing-ground of Kahalani's battalion, between Hermonit and 'Booster' ridge to the south, lay 260 Syrian tanks and hundreds of armoured personnel carriers (APCs). This area, the centre of the Syrian attack, became known to the Israelis as the 'Valley of Tears'. The Israeli victory cannot be explained by any failure of Syrian willpower. The Israelis agree that the Syrians surprised them by the strength of their fighting spirit. The Israeli advantage lay in their well-chosen firing positions and the ability of their tanks, mostly Centurions, to out-shoot the

Syrian T–55s and T–62s. Here the superior training of the Israeli tank crews was decisive. Another Israeli strength was the quality of their leadership, particularly among junior officers who often succeeded to great responsibilities as their colonels and company commanders became casualties. The Syrians executed their clearly made plans competently, but they lacked flexibility and were unable to adapt their tactics after their first failures.

Refitting on the Golan

Late on 10 October the Israeli General Staff decided to recommend that their Northern Command should continue to press the Syrian Army. After some discussion, the prime minister, Mrs Golda Meir, agreed to a limited advance in order to neutralise the Syrian Army before the mass of the Israeli war effort was swung against Egypt. Damascus was to be brought under threat of long-range artillery fire but not attacked. The Israelis had no wish to be drawn into street fighting and they also feared that a move into Damascus might trigger a Soviet intervention to save Syria.

The Israeli forces on the Golan were being refitted with all speed. Tanks were repaired and new crews found for them. Colonel Kahalani discovered, for example, that after his battalion had been reformed he knew none of his officers personally. Another battalion was largely composed of reservists from abroad. They came from 17 different countries, scarcely knew each other and many were unfamiliar with their Centurion tanks. Somehow such groups were turned into fighting units.

The Israelis crossed the old ceasefire line at 1100 on 11 October. Their three divisions were concentrated in northern Golan, on the shortest route to Damascus, even though this was also the easiest terrain for the Syrians to defend. Eitan's division began the advance on the axis Majdal Shams–Mazrat Beit Jan. This route was chosen because the impassable slopes of Mount Hermon protected the division's northern flank. Two hours

later Laner's division attacked up the main Kuneitra–Damascus road, followed by Peled's division to protect the southern flank. The 7th Brigade had discovered farmers' paths through the Syrian mine-fields and broke through their first defences, capturing the villages of Hader and Mazrat Beit Jan in the face of stiff resistance. Further south the 188th Brigade was badly mauled in an over-ambitious tank assault on the heavily defended Tel Shams position. Tel Shams was later stormed by élite paratroopers at a cost of only four wounded.

The Iraqi involvement

Laner's division advanced steadily all day, although the Syrian tank-hunting infantry counter-attacked the Israeli tank laagers, only to be driven off by a parachute battalion. Next morning, the 12th, Laner attacked again as Syrian resistance cracked. His leading brigades broke

Opposite: A knocked-out Syrian T-62, and the body of one of its crew. Syrian tank losses mounted as the Israeli defences stiffened, in spite of brave individual performances. Above: A Centurion on Golan, with bazooka side-plates removed.

out onto the plain, heading to outflank the defence lines in front of Sassa by pushing east through Knaker. As Laner scanned the plain he saw dust rising above two armoured columns advancing from the south-east. The tanks were Centurions, which suggested that this was Peled's division, but Northern Command made it clear that this was impossible. Laner checked his racing brigades and swung them to face the new threat. It was in fact the Iraqi 12th Armoured Division. The Iraqis had despatched troops to Syria as soon as the war started and they had arrived at a crucial time.

Laner deployed his four brigades in an open 'box' formation and waited for the

Iraqis. The first brush came at 1600. The Iraqis checked their advance and waited for their main body to close up. At 0300 on 13 October they incautiously pushed on, straight into Laner's box. The range was down to 200m (220yd) when the Israelis opened fire. Eighty Iraqi tanks were destroyed without loss to the Israelis.

However the momentum of the Israeli advance had been lost. The Syrians were fast making good their equipment losses as arms were poured in by the Soviet Union, even though there was little time to train the Syrian crews. Nevertheless they stabilised their position in the Sassa defences. The Iraqi force and, from 16 October, the Jordanians kept up the pressure in the south, although the three nations never succeeded in properly co-ordinating their efforts. The Israelis were content to hold their ground, making only local gains to stengthen their positions. Their attention was now concentrated on the Egyptian front. Just before Syria accepted a United Nations ceasefire on 22 October, an Israeli parachute and infantry force stormed Mount Hermon, recapturing the Israeli observation post – an extremely important last-minute gain for the IDF.

The failure of the Israeli counter-offensive on 8 October did not stop the fighting in Sinai, but for the next few days neither

side tried to make any major gains. The Egyptians made local attacks to improve their bridgehead positions and tried to wear down the Israeli tank strength using parties of missile-armed infantry. The Israelis fought back and kept their hold on the higher ground between the two main north–south roads. Meanwhile the higher commands debated their next moves, quarrelling among themselves as bitterly as the front-line troops fought each other, and Sinai was to be the area of decision.

The Israelis on the advance.
Top: Crew baggage attached to the turret during the advance.
Above: Dawn inspection and an early start. Opposite above:
A Centurion with a 0.5 inch Browning mounted up front.
Opposite below: A casualty of IDF attacks, a T-54/55 blazes fiercely.

The Egyptians disagreed about whether to put the second phase of their plan into action and push towards the Passes. General Shazli was adamant that his troops should not leave their defensive positions. General Ismail, the Minister of War, faced other pressures and, as the Syrian position worsened, he ordered Shazli to move the bulk of the Egyptian armour across the Canal for a major offensive. Despite his subordinate's pleas he would postpone it only until 14 October.

On the Israeli side, the chief of staff, General Elazar, had tried to impose order on his quarrelling generals by appointing a new commander. Gonen was not relieved, but Lieutenant-General Chaim Bar-Lev was appointed as the chief of staff's personal representative, with full authority in Sinai. Bar-Lev found a basic disagreement among his subordinates. Some, led by Sharon, wanted to attack immediately into the gap between the two Egyptian armies and, following the pre-war plan, cross the Canal. The majority agreed with Gonen that this was too dangerous until the Egyptian armour had been committed and defeated. Sharon was still thinking in terms of the battles of 1956 and 1967; the rest had a new respect for the Egyptians. There were still a thousand Egyptian tanks west of the Canal, more than enough to crush an Israeli bridgehead before it could be consolidated. On the whole Bar-Lev sided with Gonen and twice asked that Sharon be dismissed. However this was refused because of the political consequences of sacking a general who was also a leading member of the Opposition.

Timing the Israeli attack

Bar-Lev began to plan an attack and a crossing, withdrawing Adan's division from the line to prepare for it. Timing was the crucial problem. Elazar wanted to wait for the Egyptian offensive. Moshe Dayan, the Minister of Defence, was very pessimistic about the whole plan and the decision was passed to the War Cabinet. There the arguments were resolved on 12 October when intelligence reports

indicated that the Egyptian armour was at last crossing into Sinai. The attack was to be postponed until after the tank battle.

The Egyptians had brought their 21st Armoured Division and about half the 4th Armoured Division across the Canal. There were also about seven mobile SA–6 batteries in Sinai but calibration problems meant that they could not provide effective air defence for the attacking forces. The offensive began at dawn on Sunday 14 October with an intense artillery barrage, followed by advances along the main east–west roads. In the north the 18th Infantry Division, reinforced with a brigade of T–62 tanks, thrust along the coast road towards Baluza and Romani. Helicopters landed commandos in the marshes to protect the northern flank. The main Egyptian attack lay in the centre, towards the strategic crossroads at Tasa. The reinforced 2nd Infantry Division struck along the Ismailiya–Tasa axis, with the 21st Armoured Division attacking from Deversoir to Tasa. South of the Bitter Lakes, Third Army pushed a tank brigade towards the Giddi Pass while a mixed force of three brigades under 4th Armoured Division pushed south from Suez City along the coast road to Ras Sudar, then swung a tank brigade northeastwards into the mouth of the Mitla Pass. The scene was set for a massive armoured confrontation.

Tank versus tank

This was the greatest tank battle since the Second World War, and one of the largest ever. It is claimed that over 2000 tanks were involved, but this is almost certainly an exaggeration, because both sides overestimated their opponent's strength. The total involved can scarcely have exceeded 1500 tanks and it is doubtful that as many as a thousand actually saw action.

The offensive failed all along the line. The Israelis exploited their positions among the dunes, their tanks firing and moving to new positions, and they had their infantry in line with them. To deal with the Egyptian antitank teams the Israeli infantry kept up heavy machine-gun fire which was enough to distract the missile operators. This time it was the Egyptians who suffered from antitank guided weapons, as the Israelis used French SS–10 and SS–11 missiles and also the American TOW missile. The latter had only just reached Israel in a massive American airlift and the Israeli infantry had had less than a day to learn to use it.

The Egyptians suffered heavily. In the centre the leading brigade of 21st Armoured Division lost 93 tanks and the opposing Israeli brigade had only three tanks knocked out in return. The IAF was at last able to get into the battle and,

The tank battles in Sinai between 14 and 16 October were some of the biggest ever, and victory allowed the Israelis to recross the Suez Canal. Opposite: Israeli armour races across the desert. Below: M109A2 self-propelled guns, one of the main weapons the IDF developed as a result of lessons learned in 1973.

Above left: The fighting in Sinai. Israeli forces are attacking a SAM missile base while themselves under enemy fire. Above right: Success for these hard-working Israeli gunners.

The drive over the Canal

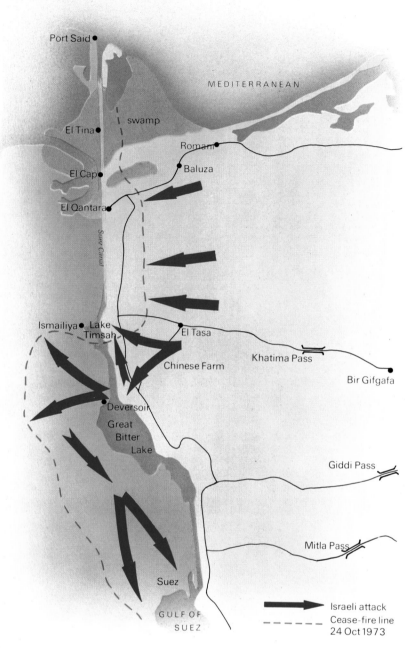

Port Said
El Tina
swamp
MEDITERRANEAN
Romani
El Cap
Baluza
El Qantara
Suez Canal
Ismailiya
Lake Timsah
El Tasa
Khatima Pass
Chinese Farm
Bir Gifgafa
Deversoir
Great Bitter Lake
Giddi Pass
Mitla Pass
Suez
GULF OF SUEZ

→ Israeli attack
----- Cease-fire line 24 Oct 1973

catching an armoured brigade of 4th Armoured Division outside the Egyptian anti-aircraft missile cover, destroyed over 60 tanks. The Israelis and Egyptians agree that the Egyptians had lost over 250 tanks by mid-morning. The Egyptians claim 50 Israeli tanks destroyed, but the Israelis admit to only 10. The shock of failure was too much for the commander of the Egyptian Second Army, General Saad Mamoun, who had a complete breakdown and took to his bed, unable to act or give orders. That evening General Bar-Lev reported to Golda Meir, 'It has been a good day. Our forces are

themselves again and so are the Egyptians'.

The Israeli crossing of the Canal

The Israelis were now ready to risk a crossing of the Suez Canal. They lacked the range of modern bridging equipment which the Egyptians had acquired from the Soviets, but they had made some preparations before the war. Their equipment included reconditioned French-built Gillois amphibious ferries and rafts built to their own design which had to be towed by tanks. Both could be used to

ferry tanks in ones and twos or linked to form a floating bridge. They had also built a 180m (200yd) bridge on rollers which could be towed, by 16 tanks, to the Canal. After the usual arguments it was decided that Sharon's division would cross first and establish a bridgehead in the Deversoir area. Adan would then cross and break out to the south-west, trapping the Third Army at Suez.

The operation began at 1700 on 15 October when one of Sharon's brigades launched a diversionary attack between Ismailia and Deversoir. Then Colonel Amnon Reshef's brigade moved into the gap between the two Egyptian armies south of Deversoir. They reached the Great Bitter Lake and swung north behind the Egyptian defences, reaching the chosen crossing area at Matzmed, opposite Deversoir, without opposition by 2100.

Now it was essential to clear the main road back to Tasa, along which all the bridging equipment had to pass. Two companies moved east, to clear the road, but they immediately came under fire from Egyptian positions south of the road, in the so-called 'Chinese Farm'. Another strong Egyptian position was revealed north of the road. Meanwhile a parachute brigade had followed Reshef's route and begun crossing in rubber assault boats. By dawn 750 men were on the west bank.

The rest of the Israeli plan had failed. The rafts and bridges were stuck in a traffic jam outside Tasa, although some Gillois ferries managed to move across country and get a handful of tanks to the west bank. Sharon wanted to continue the crossing with these ferries but Bar-Lev and Gonen insisted that he and Adan should concentrate on clearing the Tasa road and completing a proper bridge first. However the Israeli tanks and mechanised infantry could not deal with the Egyptian antitank teams which were positioned in irrigation ditches. It was midnight on the 16th before a parachute battalion could be brought forward to clear out the ditches. Just before dawn Adan managed to rush a convoy of rafts to the Canal and soon afterwards the Israelis had a bridge over it. Now the armour could get into action.

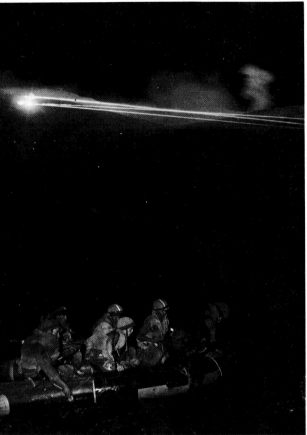

Opposite: The Israeli crossing of the Suez Canal. Below: An Israeli M-48 American-made tank crosses the Canal into Egypt. The bridge has been damaged and a tank-mounted bridge laid over the gap. Right: Israeli commandos cross the Canal under cover of darkness. Above: The peace negotiations tent at Kilometre 101 in Egypt.

The Egyptians strike back

However, the Egyptians had begun to react. On learning of the crossing on 16 October Shazli had wanted to bring his armoured formations back across the Canal to crush the Israeli bridgehead. But Ismail refused to allow any withdrawal and ordered a pincer attack on the east bank to cut the Israeli corridor to the Canal and restore the Egyptian front. The 16th Infantry and 21st Armoured Divisions tried to advance southwards but were held at bay by the brigades on the Israelis' northern perimeter. The Egyptian 25th Tank Brigade had been ordered up from the Third Army area but its approach was noted by the Israelis in time for them to deploy their reserves. The Egyptians were attacked on

Above and right: The American aid to Israel in the later stages of the Yom Kippur War included F-4E Phantoms, aircraft that were tried and proven in both an air-superiority and a ground-support role.

three sides, so that the brigade was pinned against the Great Bitter Lake and annihilated.

During 17 October the Israelis had decided that Sharon must concentrate on securing the route to the Canal while Adan's division would begin operations on the west bank. But Sharon was unwilling to give way and it took all night for Adan to extricate his forces and get two brigades to the other side. The small Israeli force which crossed on 16 October had managed to destroy several SAM sites, so opening a gap in the Egyptian air defence. Thus Adan was able to advance with air support, burst through the farmland along the Sweetwater Canal, which was a few kilometres east of the Suez Canal, and drive south. He seized the Geneifa Hills, key ground on the road to Suez. On the 19th he was joined by Brigadier-General Kalman Magen's division while Sharon at last crossed the Canal and pushed northwards.

In the Egyptian High Command, Shazli was becoming even more insistent that forces must be withdrawn to the west bank. However Sadat would not weaken his hold on Sinai, which was so vital to Egypt's diplomatic position. Shazli was close to nervous collapse when Sadat ordered his relief by General Abdel Ghani Gamasy. Obviously these dis-

agreements at the highest level were not helping the Egyptian Army. Sadat was sufficiently worried to ask the Soviet Union to convene the UN Security Council in the hope of obtaining a ceasefire.

The call for a ceasefire

The Israelis were determined to complete their operation before a ceasefire could be imposed, to ensure that they had something to bargain against the Egyptian holdings in Sinai. Adan's and Magen's divisions charged forward. On 22 October Magen cut the Cairo–Suez road and Adan reached the Canal north of Suez City. The Third Army was now trapped with only a couple of day's supplies. But the Security Council had called for a ceasefire by 1852 hours on the same day, the 22nd. After an uneasy night's peace, fighting started again on 23 October. Each side blamed the other for starting it, although the Israelis had more to gain from renewed fighting.

By dawn on 24 October Magen's troops had reached the sea in the Gulf of Suez, completing the encirclement of Suez City. Adan probed into the city, but his first tank column was ambushed and he lost over 20 tanks. Suez proved to be defended by a well-organised militia

and the Israelis had no plans for a house-to-house battle. The fighting petered out between 25 and 28 October, when the first United Nations observers arrived.

Diplomatic action and the superpowers

Before October 1973 both the Arabs and Israel believed that any future war was likely to be cut short by a ceasefire forced by the superpowers. In fact in the *Shovach Yonim* plan the Israeli Army had assumed that it might have as little as 48 hours in which to achieve its objectives before a ceasefire was imposed. The Egyptian plan for Operation Badr relied on the Soviet Union to persuade the United States to put pressure on Israel to accept a ceasefire which would include Egyptian occupation of part of Sinai. As we have seen, the United Nations did eventually manage to achieve a ceasefire, although it took rather longer than prewar plans had imagined.

At the start of the war both superpowers had tried to establish a ceasefire. For a week Henry Kissinger, the American Secretary of State, tried to limit the damage the war might do to superpower détente and to American relations with the Arabs by keeping the supply of arms to Israel to a trickle. Kissinger particularly

An Israeli F-4E with distinctive 'sharkmouth' markings.

feared that the Arabs might cut American oil supplies if the United States was seen to be responsible for an Israeli success, and he assumed that Israel would win a quick victory. The Soviets were equally convinced that Israel would win and although they immediately began to send arms to Egypt and Syria, they also tried to stop the war. According to Sadat, the Soviets tried to trick him into breaking off the war on the first day, by telling him that the Syrians had asked for a ceasefire. But once it became clear that all was not well with Israel, the Soviets saw the advantages to be gained from conspicuously supporting the victorious Arabs and a massive airlift of supplies began, supplemented by merchant ships.

US aid to Israel

As the United States came to appreciate Israel's difficulties, its policy changed. In Kissinger's words, 'We tried to talk in the first week. When that didn't work, we said, fine, we'll start pouring in equipment until we create a new reality.' The American Military Airlift Command began its airlift on 13 October using C–5 and C–141 transports. In a month 22,665 tonnes had been flown in, and the Soviets had delivered similar quantities to the Arabs. The American airlift included the replacement of items such as M–60 and M–48 tanks, 155mm and 175mm self-propelled guns, helicopters, ammunition and aircraft parts. New weapons such as TOW antitank missiles, radar or laser-guided 'smart bombs' and Electronic Counter Measures (ECM) equipment were included, and Skyhawk and Phantom aircraft were flown directly to Israel from the United States.

The American action persuaded the Arabs to use the 'oil weapon' which had been discussed before the war. On 16 October the Arab oil producers met in Kuwait. They increased their prices by 70% and next day announced a 5% cut in production, to be followed by a 5% cut each month until the Israeli-occupied territories were freed and the Palestinians restored to their homeland. As American aid to Israel increased, Arab oil action concentrated on the United States and by 22 October all the Arab nations had put an embargo on American supplies. In the short term the oil weapon had little influence on events, but eventually it had serious consequences. America's allies in Europe and Japan adopted a more pro-Arab line, referring to Israel's occupation of Arab territory in 1967 as illegal. This strained relations between America and the allies. The other and even more serious effect of the oil weapon came in December when the oil exporters increased prices by 128%, which led to general inflation and weakened the world economy.

The main superpower clash during the war came after the first UN ceasefire broke down. Egypt appealed to America and Russia to 'maintain' the ceasefire. America refused, but on 24 October Brezhnev hinted to Nixon that Russia might act unilaterally. American intelligence warned that Soviet airborne divisions had been alerted for an intervention. Nixon ordered the highest state of nuclear alert, *Defcon–3*, and the Sixth Fleet, already concentrated in the eastern Mediterranean, deployed to battle positions threatening the airborne divisions' route to the Middle East. The Soviets signalled a softer line by agreeing to

superpower involvement in the United Nations ceasefire monitoring force and tensions relaxed. However the crisis did lead America's allies to complain about the lack of consultation before the alert was called.

The lessons of the war

Immediately the war was over, the media rushed to discover the military lessons which might emerge. It was confidently announced that the age of the tank and the manned aircraft had ended; the missile era was beginning. Writers claimed that 'blitzkrieg was dead'. Ten years after the war it is clear that much of the early analysis was wildly false, being based on inadequate statistics and a failure to consider the tactical setting of the actions from which the statistics were drawn.

Of the total Israeli aircraft losses, 40% occurred in the first 48 hours of the war. These amounted to 14% of IAF front-line strength. But in this period Israel deliberately chose to sacrifice her air force in order to hold the line on the ground, particularly in the Golan. Aircraft were used for close air support at once, and resources were not allocated to suppressing the enemy air defences first. Once the crisis had passed, the IAF adopted more normal tactics and casualties were dramatically reduced.

In the entire war Israeli losses per sortie were less than in 1967, when air power was considered triumphant. Israel lost just over 100 aircraft. Over 40% were shot down by anti-aircraft artillery, especially the ZSU–23–4 radar-controlled, short-range cannon system; under 40% were lost to SA–2 and SA–3 missiles and

less than 10% to the SA–6. During the whole war only 1·5% of Arab missiles fired succeeded in destroying their target. The shoulder-fired SA–7 was particularly disappointing; over 5000 were fired, but only four aircraft were destroyed. Many more Israeli aircraft were actually hit but they were recovered and often repaired. On the Arab side total losses were 480 aircraft, 55% of which were shot down in air-to-air combat. Between 15% and 20% of Arab casualties were caused by their own fire.

Pilots or drones?

These figures do not suggest that the manned aircraft is finished, particularly as the experience of 1973 has led air forces to develop new counters to ground-based air defences. But the consequence has been to increase the complexity and therefore the cost of aircraft. The Israelis have led the way in developing pilotless drones for use in high-risk missions, such as reconnaissance along the front line. Drones are also used to divert missile fire from manned aircraft. There is general agreement that aircraft are best employed in striking deep behind the enemy's front line but air forces knew this before the war started.

A similar story can be told about the tank's demise. Taking the figures for both sides, the most effective antitank weapon was undoubtedly the tank; well over half the tank kills were credited to other tanks. This was particularly true in confused, close-range battles where the tank's ability to engage different targets in quick succession was often crucial. The Israelis did suffer heavily from Sagger missiles and RPG–7 rockets in the early days of the war, but it was their own disastrous tactics, rather than the virtues of Arab weapons, which made their losses so heavy. Over-confidence led to the neglect of basic lessons which other armies had been absorbing since the Second World War. Since 1973 the Israelis have fallen into line with the rest, relying on all-arms combat teams rather than units made up exclusively of tanks. The Yom Kippur War did demonstrate the effectiveness of some defensive systems, particularly when allied to suitable terrain, but several episodes also suggest that properly organised and handled forces are still capable of successful offensive action, with the tank having a key role in both attack and defence.

A question of cost

Many other lessons can be drawn from the war, although it is vital to be careful in applying them to other theatres of operation, where different terrain or climate could invalidate them. Helicopters were found to be vulnerable near the front line, but invaluable in transport roles in rear areas. The flexibility of self-propelled artillery was clearly demonstrated on the Israeli side. At sea Israeli missile-armed patrol boats won control of the Mediterranean coastline.

The war also made it clear that expenditure rates of modern weapons are extremely high. Not only is it essential to maintain much larger stockpiles in peacetime, but at the tactical level it is significant that the new Israeli tank, the Merkava, has a very large and easily reloaded ammunition compartment, in order to reduce the time the tanks must spend out of action. The psychological stress of modern operations, which involve days of continuous fighting, was generally apparent. Of Israeli casualties, 10% were caused by battle shock, though the recovery rate was high and surprisingly rapid. But most of all the war re-emphasised the basic truths which any war teaches, such as the value of training, and, despite the increasing sophistication of weapon systems, the importance of the morale of the man behind the weapon.

The consequences of the war

Despite early set-backs, the achievement of the IDF was impressive. In the Golan the Israelis more than made good their early losses of territory. The appearance of their forces on the African shore of the Suez Canal was a remarkable performance. In military terms the war can in no way be described as an Israeli defeat. But the image of those first disasters was a lasting one, not just in the eyes of the world but also inside Israel itself. The bubble of Israeli over-confidence had been burst and Israel was less inclined to

rely solely on her own forces for her security. The war caused stresses with the IDF and Israeli society itself which are still being felt.

The war therefore represented an Arab success, boosting Arab prestige in the world. This success possibly helped to give the Arabs the confidence at last to assert the power they hold by owning so much of the world's oil resources. In particular the war was a success for President Sadat, enabling him to end his dependence on the Soviet Union and begin a new relationship with the United States. However, when this was not followed immediately by improvements in Egypt's domestic position but rather led to Egyptian isolation in the Arab world, Sadat's position was fatally compromised. The Yom Kippur War was not the 'war to end wars' in the Middle East. There was more conflict still to come.

Opposite above: An Israeli Phantom prepares to make a low-level strike in Sinai.
Above: Israeli prisoners, about to be filmed for propaganda purposes.
Below: The great question raised by the war was whether Sagger antitank missiles like the one mounted on a BMP here had made the tank too vulnerable to rule the battlefield.
Inset: The result of the new antitank weapons – a knocked-out Israeli M-48.

9. The Crisis of Islam

Arab euphoria and new-found unity was destined to survive for only a short while in the period after the Yom Kippur War of October 1973. One of the most striking aspects of that conflict had been the way in which the oil producers of the Gulf had displayed their solidarity with the Arab cause by introducing sanctions against their pro-Israeli customers. This did not last. Although the Western Europeans and Japanese did suffer some distress from the induced shortage of oil, the main target of the sanctions – the United States– was able to weather the storm. There may have been a slight shift in attitudes towards the Arab-Israeli dispute, but in the main the oil weapon did not have the intended effect. Some Arab oil undoubtedly 'leaked out' and reached the West but more importantly the international system of oil distribution, managed by the oil companies themselves, spread the burden of hardship more evenly through the consumer market. Finally, as Western states tightened their belts and reduced their demand for oil, the Gulf producers found themselves in possession of a glut of what had once been a scarce commodity. Their attempt to create a united Arab front quickly turned into a nightmare.

Of far more importance, however, was the split which occurred between Egypt and Syria. Despite their common purpose during the Yom Kippur War, the move by President Sadat towards a peace settlement with Israel in the mid-1970s placed the two Arab countries on opposite sides of the superpower divide. As Syria looked to the Soviet Union for support and arms, Egypt's foreign policy leaned more and more towards the West, particularly as Sadat's decisions led to his virtual isolation in the Arab world.

Sadat's peace policy

The reasons for this dramatic *volte face* are not difficult to appreciate. The Yom Kippur War had restored Egyptian military honour and dignity, even though the armed forces had suffered heavily in the process. For Egypt there was no more to be gained from further use of military power, so Sadat entered into bilateral negotiations with Israel in an effort to exploit the new-found reputation of his forces. Although an essential element of the 'joint war strategy' of 1973 had been a tacit understanding that all subsequent negotiations over territory would be made in conjunction with the Syrians, Sadat realised that the national interests of Egypt had to take precedence. The Egyptian people had become increasingly aware that their country, which had always had only a limited stake in the struggle with Israel, was nevertheless shouldering the heaviest burden. The years of struggle, with their massive expenditure on defence, had pauperised the Egyptian economy while others in the Arab world had amassed huge fortunes through the sale of oil. For a country which desired to be rid of the war and the Palestinians, Sadat's pursuit of peace enjoyed plenty of grass-roots support. In 1975 he entered into a formal disengagement agreement with the Israelis which in time returned to Egypt all that was economically useful in Sinai. The Suez Canal was cleared of war debris and accumulated silt by the Americans and British, and began to operate once

Below: A young Palestinian armed with an AKMS assault rifle. Opposite: The problem of world oil supplies.

Oil from the Middle East-1978

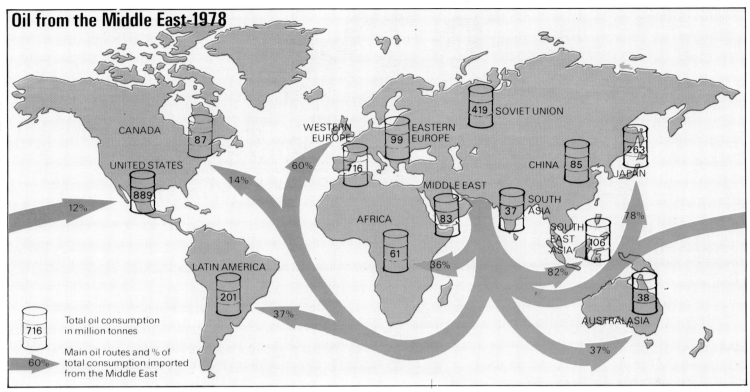

716   Total oil consumption in million tonnes

60%   Main oil routes and % of total consumption imported from the Middle East

The Middle East oil supply-1978

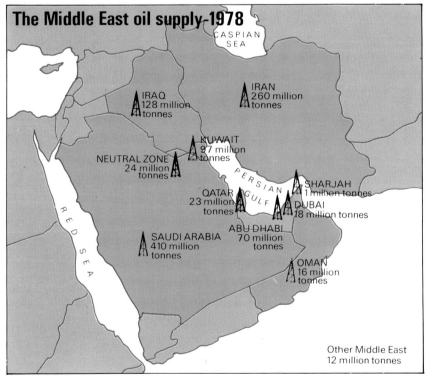

CASPIAN SEA

IRAQ
128 million tonnes

IRAN
260 million tonnes

KUWAIT
97 million tonnes

NEUTRAL ZONE
24 million tonnes

PERSIAN GULF

SHARJAH
1 million tonnes

QATAR
23 million tonnes

DUBAI
18 million tonnes

SAUDI ARABIA
410 million tonnes

ABU DHABI
70 million tonnes

OMAN
16 million tonnes

RED SEA

Other Middle East
12 million tonnes

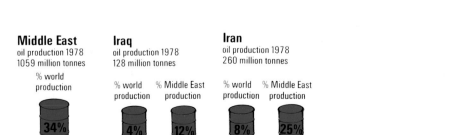

Middle East
oil production 1978
1059 million tonnes

% world production

34%

Iraq
oil production 1978
128 million tonnes

% world production 4%

% Middle East production 12%

Iran
oil production 1978
260 million tonnes

% world production 8%

% Middle East production 25%

again, to the benefit of the Egyptian economy, in 1976. At the same time, the Canal cities, administered by the UN since 1973, returned to Egyptian jurisdiction, and the western part of Sinai, from the Canal to the Mitla Pass, was handed back to give the country a useful buffer-zone.

The style and manner of the negotiations were very much a reflection of Sadat – spectacular, highly personalised and with little prior consultation. In 1977 he journeyed to Israel and addressed the *Knesset* (Israel's parliament), a move which scandalised the Arab world. In September 1978 he met with the Israeli prime minister, Menachem Begin, under the 'chairmanship' of US President Jimmy Carter in the Camp David peace talks.

The tragedy for Sadat was that Begin and the Israelis were not prepared to match his bravery and embark on a genuine peace initiative. Instead they preferred to pursue a policy which had more limited goals. Begin bargained territory in Sinai in exchange for American security guarantees but was not prepared to address the fundamental issue of a Palestinian homeland. He used the Camp David negotiations to appease American criticism of Israeli intransigence and at the same time enhanced Israeli security by stabilising the Sinai border.

Peace with Cairo took Egypt out of the Arab front line and allowed the Israelis to concentrate their military resources against the Syrians and Palestinians in Lebanon.

Nevertheless Camp David did produce a peace of sorts because it removed the most powerful state from the Arab alignment. Sadat had hoped that Israeli promises to link any agreement over Sinai to similar ones over the West Bank and East Jerusalem would be sufficient to secure the support of the moderates in the Arab camp. Instead, 17 members of the Arab League condemned Sadat, and Egypt found herself increasingly a pariah in the Middle East. Only Morocco and the Sudanese Republic gave Sadat any measure of support.

Egyptian isolation

The opposition from Saudi Arabia was particularly disastrous for Sadat and the Americans. The Saudis were outraged by Sadat's surrender of what they saw as the most precious bargaining counter – recognition of Israel – without achieving

While the Arab world split apart, Israel built up her arsenals. The Merkava tank (above and below) demonstrated Israeli self-sufficiency. Politics in the Arab world became even less coherent when, in December 1979, the Soviet Union invaded the Islamic state of Afghanistan. Opposite: A Soviet sentry at an Afghan checkpoint. Opposite inset left: Mohammed Taraki, president of Afghanistan April 1977 to March 1979, when he was replaced by Hafizullah Amin (inset centre) who was replaced by Babrak Kamal (inset right) after the Soviet invasion.

anything of substance in return. Ever since the death of Nasser in 1970 the corner-stone of Saudi policy had been to forge a moderate Arab consensus on a whole range of issues, from the Palestinian problem to the oil policies of the Organisation of Arab Petroleum Exporting Countries (OAPEC) and regional disputes. A central theme of this policy had been an attempt to establish links with the more radical Arab states and thus deny the Soviets a role in the Middle East. Prior to Camp David no Arab capital was on speaking terms with as many other Arab capitals as Riyadh. Sadat destroyed that consensus and allowed the Soviets to make further inroads by alienating the United States from the mainstream of Middle Eastern affairs.

Even as the Camp David talks staggered towards a confused conclusion, attention was already shifting elsewhere, to what Zbigniew Brzezinski, President Carter's security adviser, described as the 'arc of crisis' in the Islamic world. Pakistan had become increasingly troubled and was ruled by a repressive military regime. To the north lay Afghanistan, where Soviet-sponsored coups had exacerbated the problems of government over one of the world's most unruly tribal societies. Neighbouring Turkey had been a staunch member of NATO but was torn by religious unrest and social instabilities.

To the south lay Saudi Arabia, whose monarchy, hitherto invulnerable, was beginning to look fragile. In 1975 King Feisal was assassinated and replaced by his brother Khalid; in 1979 religious fanatics seized the Great Mosque in Mecca and held it for two weeks in protest at the 'corruption' of Saudi Arabian society. Egypt was kept from bankruptcy by American handouts while Sudan barely survived the repeated attempts at coups launched from fanatical Libya. In Ethiopia the junta was sustained by Soviet aid and the presence of some 17,000 Cubans, having switched from a pro-American stance in order to fight a bitter war against Somalia in 1977–78. But the centre of gravity in the 'arc of crisis' was non-Arab Iran. It was the world's fourth-largest producer of oil and for two decades Washington's most prestigious client, a citadel of military and economic strength in the Middle East.

The Shah, one of the last of the world's great absolute monarchs, sought to create a technological super-state funded by petro-dollars. In 1978 this grandiose scheme collapsed before a resurgence of Islamic fundamentalism. The Shi'ite Mullahs – the traditional conscience of the nation – were scandalised by the new consumer society that had emerged. The extravagance of the new élite, the undermining of traditional values and the corruption of the Royal Family were all blamed on the considerable American presence in Iran. Instead of seeking accommodation with the nation's spiritual leaders, the Shah chose confrontation and then – in 1979 – to exile them. It is perhaps ironic that the Ayatollah Khom-

Above: The Iranian-Iraqi border.

eini should have used modern technology – the telephone from his Paris exile and the cassette tape recorder – to broadcast his message of old Islam to the universities and Mosques. By the time the Shah had realised his mistake and sought reconciliation, it was too late.

The Ayatollah Khomeini

The decline of the Shah and his exile coincided with the return of the Ayatollah in triumph and the creation of a violently anti-Western Islamic Republic. Turmoil and revolutionary fervour challenged the basic principles of international diplomacy when an excess of mob violence led to the storming of the US Embassy in Tehran in November 1979 and the ordeal of the hostages, which was to last until January 1981.

Even while the United States and the new Reagan administration of 1981 were grappling with the problems of a Soviet war in Afghanistan, the Gulf and Iran, their Middle East policy suffered another grievous blow. On 6 October 1981 President Sadat of Egypt was assassinated by his own soldiers, an extreme faction of the Moslem Brotherhood, as he took the

salute at a parade to celebrate the victorious crossing of the Suez Canal eight years earlier.

Sadat's policies towards Israel, in challenging the most sacred values of Arab opinion, had effectively isolated him in the Arab world. What sealed his doom, however, was the loss of public support inside Egypt. In domestic affairs he had moved away from the state socialism introduced by Nasser and towards private enterprise and encouragement of Western investment. Such policies were of benefit to those who could afford the consumer boom, but did little to help the poor and aroused the wrath of 'the faithful'. Islamic fundamentalism spread and the Moslem Brotherhood gained fresh recruits.

Other Arab leaders had reason to shrink before the onslaught of Shi'ite fundamentalism. Many states were ruled by leaders who came from the Sunn'ite sect, though they had large numbers of Shi'ites amongst their populations. Tension mounted in the Gulf as the Ayatollah

called on the Shi'ites to rise up and overthrow their Sunn'ite masters.

The immediate focus of religious tension lay between Iran and its neighbour Iraq. Animosity between the two peoples stretches back for a millennium and longer. It is reputed to have begun in the seventh century when the Arab armies of the Caliph Omar routed the Persian hordes at the Battle of Qadisiyeh.

In recent times tension has focused on a number of issues. The Shatt al-Arab waterway, which is formed by the confluence of the Tigris and Euphrates rivers, provides the border between the states. The waterway is navigable for some 100km (62 miles) and has become the main outlet for Iraqi oil. In 1937 Britain, acting in the interests of Iraq, persuaded the Persians (Iranians) to accept the low-water mark on the eastern (i.e. Persian) shore as the actual border. This gave Iraq virtual control over the movement of all shipping. So long as Iraq was ruled by the Hashemites this was not a problem, but after General Kassim's coup in 1958 the ideological rift focused on this issue as Iran demanded a reversion to the median line (i.e. an imaginary line down the middle of the river) as the official border.

The Kurdish question

The Kurdish question has been another cause for friction and conflict between the states. The Kurds have a national history which predates Islam. They are a pastoral, tribal society who inhabit the largely inaccessible region of the Zagros Mountains or 'Kurdistan' which lies astride south-eastern Turkey, western Iran and northern Iraq. First conquered by the Arabs in the seventh century, the Kurds have accepted Islam but not the Arabs. Twice in modern times the Kurds have come close to achieving self-determination and national independence. The first occasion was immediately after the First World War when the Turkish Empire was dismembered, the second more recently in 1945 when the Soviets sponsored a Kurdish Republic of Azerbaijan and secession from Persia.

Below: Signing the Camp David accords. Below right: Kurdish irregulars. Right: The Ayatollah Khomeini

Ever since, the Kurds, under the leadership of Mullah Mustafa Barzani, have sought to break away from Iraqi control. Between 1961 and 1975 there was an almost perpetual state of conflict which absorbed much of the military energies and budget of Iraq. The Iranians supplied the Kurds with arms in order both to embarrass the radical government of Baghdad and as a lever to persuade the Iraqis to agree to a revision of the border. In 1975 the Iraqis accepted OAPEC mediation and at the Treaty of Baghdad reluctantly submitted to the Iranian claims over the Shatt al-Arab. The Iranians for their part abandoned the Kurds to their fate. The Iraqis went over to the offensive and the Kurds were forced to flee into exile or submit to the will of Baghdad.

The president of Iraq, Saddam Hussein Takriti, sees himself as the modern Nasser in the Arab world. Since coming to power in 1979 he has used the impressive oil revenues of the state to build up the military and economic power of Iraq to challenge for the role of the great power in the Gulf. The retreat of the British from all their previous influence in the region (with the possible exception of Oman) left a vacuum which Saddam Hussein sought to fill. He demanded the Iranians should return the strategically important Abu Musa and Tanb Islands which lie close to the Straits of Hormuz, allow self-determination to the Arabs in

the oil-rich Iranian province of Khuzestan, and agree to a revision of the Baghdad Treaty of 1975. In the face of such demands, relations between the two states deteriorated rapidly. The Ayatollah responded by calling upon the Shi'ites in Iraq, who formed the majority of the population, to overthrow Saddam Hussein and his Sunn'ite government.

The Gulf War

On 17 September 1980 Iraq took the formal step of 'cancelling' the Treaty of Baghdad and the armies on both sides mobilised. After four days of artillery exchanges Iraqi divisions, in some instances spearheaded by Iranian exiles, stormed across the border. The Iraqis

publicised their grievances with Iran but their real war aims were to inflict a massive military defeat on the Islamic Republic and so topple the regime.

There were some critical flaws in the war plan which became increasingly evident as the conflict developed. Saddam Hussein had counted on the Iranian Army having disintegrated since the fall of the Shah to a point where it was no longer effective in combat. Though the Iraqis made some gains they clearly misjudged the impact of the war on the Iranian population, who quickly united behind their leader and supported the armed forces in the battle. The Iraqis also threw away their advantages in mobility and armour when they became embroiled in a fight for the cities. They laid siege to Khorramshahr and Abadan where the hastily mobilised Islamic Guard defended with fanatical fervour and denied victory to the Iraqi regular formations.

By the autumn of 1980 the Iraqi offensive had stalled and, as the rains fell, the army was forced onto the defensive. While both sides regrouped, other Middle Eastern states tried to mediate, but in vain. The greater strength and resources of Iran told in her favour and throughout 1981 the Iranians gradually recaptured the initiative and much of the territory they had lost in the first months of the war. Massed infantry assaults, with support from some armour and artillery, pushed the Iraqis back and in September 1981 the Iranians lifted the siege of Abadan. The Iraqis counter-attacked in the Qasr-e-Shirin sector but they were repulsed with heavy casualties.

Throughout 1982 both sides looked for outside support and fresh supplies of arms

Above: Photographs of the Ayatollah Khomeini displayed by the post-revolutionary Iranian Army. Right: Mortars in action in the early stage of the fighting in the Gulf War.

and equipment. Iran turned to the Soviet bloc and those Middle Eastern states who had no love for Saddam Hussein, including Israel, Syria and Libya. The Soviets backed both camps and Iraq found support from Egypt where Sadat's successor, President Husni Mubarak, was seeking to rehabilitate his country into the Arab fold. Jordan was enthusiastically pro-Iraqi and in January 1982 King Hussein raised the 'Yarmuk Brigade' to fight alongside Saddam Hussein's forces.

The Iranian counter-offensive

The Iranians, with their superior Western weapons, were ready to launch a major offensive before the Iraqis and in March 1982 attacked the Dezful sector where their enemies were still regrouping. They shrugged off some weak spoiling attacks by the Iraqi Fourth Army and with a force of 100,000 men, including Islamic Guards and an armoured division redeployed from the Pakistani frontier, penetrated deep into Iraqi-held territory. In the course of some bitter fighting the

The major areas of fighting

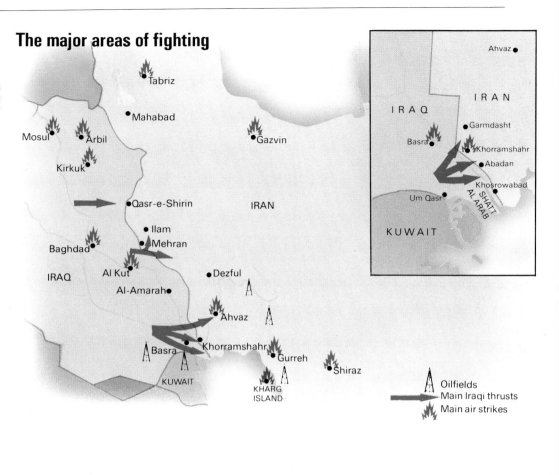

Oilfields
Main Iraqi thrusts
Main air strikes

Above: The refineries at Abadan ablaze. Right: Iraqi infantry prepare to go into action with a rocket launcher. Above right: The initial Iraqi offensives.

The Entebbe Raid

At noon on Sunday, 27 June 1976, Air France flight 139, carrying 256 passengers and 12 crew members from Tel Aviv to Paris, took off from Athens airport after a refuelling stop. Eight minutes later four terrorists – two from the West German Baader-Meinhof group and two from the Popular Front for the Liberation of Palestine – took over the aircraft. They forced the pilot to divert to Benghazi in Libya and then, after taking on more fuel, to fly south to Entebbe in Uganda. The hijackers, joined on the ground by other Palestinians and openly supported by the Ugandan Army of dictator Idi Amin, herded the hostages into a disused terminal building. On 29 June, Uganda Radio broadcast the demands – in exchange for the hostages, 53 convicted terrorists were to be released from gaols in Israel, West Germany, Kenya, Switzerland and France.

From the start, it was the Israelis who were under pressure. Of the hostages, over 100 were Israeli citizens and, as reports filtered out of Entebbe that they were being segregated from the other passengers, it was obvious that the hijackers were determined to force the government of Yitzhak Rabin to taste the humiliation of public surrender to their demands. The pressure was increased on 30 June when the non-Israeli hostages were released and a deadline of 4 July imposed: if Rabin did not give in by then, the remaining hostages would be shot.

But Israel had a tradition of responding harshly to acts of terrorism and, as the deadline approached, a rescue plan was hurriedly formulated. Presented to the Cabinet on 1 July, it proposed that 200 specially selected paratroopers should be flown in secret to Entebbe in four C–130 Hercules transports to storm the terminal building and release the hostages. It would be a risky venture – the distance by air from southern Israel to Entebbe is over 4000km (2500 miles) and the Hercules would be operating at the extreme of their

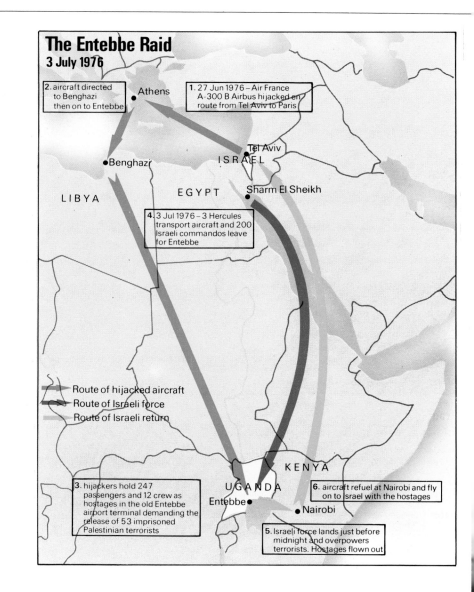

The Entebbe Raid
3 July 1976

2. aircraft directed to Benghazi then on to Entebbe

Athens

1. 27 Jun 1976 – Air France A-300 B Airbus hijacked en route from Tel Aviv to Paris

Tel Aviv

ISRAEL

● Benghazi

LIBYA

EGYPT

Sharm El Sheikh

4. 3 Jul 1976 – 3 Hercules transport aircraft and 200 Israeli commandos leave for Entebbe

Route of hijacked aircraft
Route of Israeli force
Route of Israeli return

KENYA

3. hijackers hold 247 passengers and 12 crew as hostages in the old Entebbe airport terminal demanding the release of 53 imprisoned Palestinian terrorists

UGANDA

Entebbe ●

6. aircraft refuel at Nairobi and fly on to Israel with the hostages

● Nairobi

5. Israeli force lands just before midnight and overpowers terrorists. Hostages flown out

range – but with no alternative available, the gamble had to be taken. The force took off from Sharm el Sheikh, the southerly tip of Sinai, at 1530 on Saturday, 3 July.

The first Hercules arrived over Entebbe in the middle of a rainstorm at 2301 hours and landed immediately behind a scheduled commercial airliner. The Ugandans were taken completely by surprise, enabling the advance force of paras, commanded by Lieutenant-Colonel Jonathan ('Yoni') Netanyahu, to disembark in a dark corner of the airfield. They stormed the terminal building as the hostages were asleep, killing seven

armed terrorists and clearing the way for the other three Hercules to land. Unfortunately Netanyahu was mortally wounded by fire from a nearby control tower, but he had done his job well. Amidst significant Ugandan confusion, the rest of the para force, backed by armoured cars, attacked other airfield buildings and destroyed 11 MiG fighter aircraft parked on the runway. The 106 hostages were quickly taken on board a Hercules and by 2358 they were on their way home. It was a remarkable rescue and one which dealt a severe blow not only to the PLO but to terrorist groups worldwide.

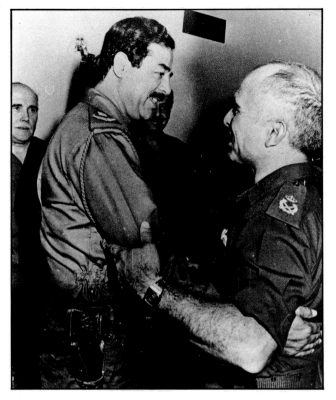

Above: Iranian M-60 tanks on their way to the front near Shiraz. Below: Ebullient Iraqi troops on the banks of the Shatt-al-Arab. Iraqi hopes of an early victory swiftly evaporated, however. Left: Iraqi leader Saddam Hussein (left) was happy to accept the help of King Hussein of Jordan in October 1980.

Iraqi 10th Armoured Division was decimated and the Iranians recaptured an estimated 200 sq. km (772 sq. miles) of territory, which took their spearheads to within 8km (5 miles) of the frontier. The Iranians paused to regroup and a month later struck again with an offensive into Khuzestan. The Iraqis had found little support from local Arabs and in the 'battle for the oil wells' fell back in some disarray. In September the Iranians recaptured Khorramshahr but their offensive stalled as the Iraqis resolutely defended their own frontier region.

On 1 November 1982 an Iranian force of 20,000 men launched a fresh offensive along an 80km (50-mile) front in the Dezful sector. The Iranians claimed to have penetrated 10km (6 miles) into Iraq, inflicted 10,000 casualties on the Iraqis and interdicted with artillery fire the strategically vital highway which links the port of Basra with Baghdad some 320km (200 miles) to the north.

It is estimated that each side has suffered more than 100,000 battle casualties and enormous damage to its economy. Iraq has repeatedly stated that it is willing to negotiate, but the chief obstacle remains Khomeini's unconditional demand that Saddam Hussein should be removed from office. Iran does have a host of other problems, however, not least a new conflict with its Kurdish population. In October 1982 the four largest Sunn'ite tribes rebelled when the Ayatollah at-

tempted to impose the Shi'ite sect on their Mosques. This conflict has all the potential of being a long-drawn-out and bloody affair.

The divisions in the Arab world

The Gulf War has divided the Arab world, with Jordan and Saudi Arabia supporting Iraq while the Syrians, PLO and Libya have sided with Iran. The Gulf States have been more concerned to limit the conflict and shore up their own defences against the Shi'ite onslaught should Iran eventually prove the victor. These states have so far failed to achieve any significant degree of collective security in their approach to the war. Though Saudi Arabia, Kuwait, Oman, Bahrain, Qatar and the United Arab Emirates did form the Gulf Cooperation Council in January 1981, the search for a defence pact has been elusive. This is caused in part by the differences in their approach to the superpowers. Kuwait is the only Gulf power with established diplomatic ties with the Soviet Union, while Oman, sensitive to its responsibilities for the strategically vital Straits of Hormuz and locked into a Western sphere of influence, refuses to break its commitments, especially to the United States over provision facilities for the Rapid Deployment Force. This, with its airmobile and amphibious capability, is now available for interventionary duties should the vital interests of the West be threatened.

The war also presented the Western world with a very public spectacle of its own particular nightmare – a major blitzkrieg among the oil wells. Though Soviet and US naval task forces 'shadow box' off the Straits of Hormuz and the West agonises on how to respond to threats from outside the NATO area, the war has had little impact on oil supplies.

Below: The arteries of the Western world lie exposed in the politically volatile Middle East. Western concern at the possible consequences of the Gulf War was intense.

Other states have compensated for the deficit and recession in the West has led to a glut of oil on the world markets. In the meantime the war continues with no sign of a negotiated or military settlement in sight.

But the problems of the Islamic world act merely as a background to the seemingly never-ending conflict between the Arabs and the Jews. In the immediate aftermath of the Yom Kippur War, as Sadat initiated and then pursued his chosen policy of peace negotiations, the security of Israel appeared to improve, particularly as the PLO, having taken little active part in the 1973 campaign, were in no position to attack the state with telling effect. But the Palestinian menace would not subside, gradually reasserting itself on the northern borders of Israel, where the confusion and political chaos of Lebanon offered a degree of sanctuary to the *fedayeen*. Throughout the decade since 1973, Lebanon has been the stage upon which possibly the most tragic scene of the Arab-Israeli dispute has been played out.

Operation Babylon

At 1500 hours (local time) on Sunday 7 June 1981, 16 Israeli fighter-bombers – eight F–15 Eagles and eight F–16 Fighting Falcons – took off from Etzion in Sinai and headed south-east in tight formation at extremely low altitude. Their mission – codenamed Operation Babylon – was top secret and dangerous: to destroy an Iraqi nuclear reactor at Al Tuwaitha, just outside Baghdad, before it became operational and gave the unpredictable regime of Saddam Hussein the capability to produce nuclear weapons for possible use against Israel. Arab possession of such weapons would fundamentally alter the balance of power in the Middle East.

Iraq had displayed interest in nuclear technology as early as 1960, signing an agreement with the Soviet Union for the building of a small research reactor which was completed in 1968. But the Soviets refused to develop this further and in an attempt to gain more powerful capability which would lead, eventually, to possession of nuclear weapons, Iraq approached the French and Italians in 1975. France proved the more amenable, helping to build two reactors at Al Tuwaitha under the Iraqi codename '17 Tammuz'. One of these – Tammuz II – was a harmless research reactor, but Tammuz I, a 70-megawatt 'Material Test Reactor' had the undoubted capacity to produce weapon-grade uranium, particularly when used in conjunction with research facilities provided by the Italians. The French theoretically controlled the supply of fuel, but by 1980 Saddam Hussein had begun to stockpile uranium ore from Brazil, Portugal and Niger, giving him effective independence. The Israelis realised the danger – indeed, in April 1979 Mossad (Israeli Intelligence) agents had sabotaged the reactor cores for Tammuz I at Toulon, as they awaited shipment to Iraq – and in October 1980, aware that Tammuz I was now close to completion, Menachem Begin's Cabinet decided to authorise a pre-emptive air strike.

The task was by no means easy. Al Tuwaitha is over 1000km (600 miles) from Israeli airbases in Sinai and although an attack from the south-west was not expected by the Iraqis, who since September 1980 had been preoccupied with their war against Iran, there was no direct route available which did not entail flying over Jordanian or Saudi Arabian territory. In addition, on 30 September 1980 two Iranian F-4 Phantoms had penetrated Iraqi air space and attacked Al Tuwaitha; the reactors were undamaged but the Iraqis had responded by substantially increasing their air defences. The Israeli plan reflected these problems. The F–16s, each armed with two 907kg (2000lb) high explosive bombs, were to act as the attacking force, protected by F–15s flying top cover, and the approach was to be made at very low altitude over the desert wastes of northern Saudi Arabia and southern Iraq. The aircraft were to maintain strict radio silence throughout and were to operate all the latest navigational and electronic countermeasures aids.

It worked perfectly. The force approached Al Tuwaitha at 1730 on 7 June and, as the F–15s climbed to provide protection, the F–16s went into the attack. The lead aircraft shattered the concrete dome of Tammuz I, exposing the reactor to remarkably precise destruction as 14 bombs entered the gaping hole. In two minutes it was all over; the F–16s climbed to rejoin the F–15s and together they flew high and fast for home, arriving back at Etzion by 1900. Tammuz I lay in ruins and with it Iraqi hopes of an early acquisition of nuclear weapons. Israel was safe for a few more years.

10. Lebanon in Flames

There is a widespread belief that the recent problems of Lebanon stem entirely from the presence within that state of Palestinian refugees and various PLO armed factions. It is undeniable that they have complicated matters and that they have triggered a series of Israeli retaliatory strikes across the Lebanese border, culminating in the all-out invasion and occupation of the southern part of the country in 1982, but underlying animosities and communal strife have been endemic in the land for centuries.

In superficial terms, the main and most obvious split within the population is between Christian and Moslem and the temptation is to cite this as a neat explanation of inter-communal conflict. In reality, however, the situation is far more complex, containing a bewildering catalogue of religions, sects and beliefs. On the 'Christian' side there are Maronite (followers of John Maron, a seventh-century monotheistic patriarch), Roman Catholic, Protestant, Greek Catholic, Greek Orthodox, Syrian Orthodox and Armenian Orthodox communities, most of which are mutually hostile. On the 'Moslem' side are the Shi'ite and Sunn'ite sects, the Druzes (followers of an eleventh-century Moslem heretic, Ismail ad-Darazi) and Alawites, while in the middle are the non-Israeli Jews, Europeans and a host of smaller groups. Nor is this the full extent of the problem, for overlaid on such divisions there is also the myriad of political factions – Phalangists (supporters of a Christian-based party with its origins in the fascism of 1930s Europe), Nasserists, pro-Syrian Ba'athists, pro-Iraqi Ba'athists, liberals, socialists, communists, conservatives, Islamic fundamentalists and simple nationalists are some of the confusing spectrum. The possible combinations which can and do exist in Lebanon are legion, even without the Palestinian dimension.

Greater Syria

This potential for internal strife is not aided by the nature of the Lebanese state. Before 1920 there was no such country, the area in question – a narrow coastal strip, overshadowed by a range of mountains which drop precipitously into the Beqaa Valley to the east – having traditionally been regarded as part of 'Greater Syria'. Indeed, for much of the period of Turkish rule from the sixteenth century, no distinction was made between the coastal region and its hinterland, although in 1864, under pressure from the pro-Maronite French, the Turkish rulers were obliged to afford special protection to the predominantly Christian area around Mount Lebanon.

French interest in the trading potential of the region reached its apogee at the end of the First World War, when the area of Greater Syria was detached from the Turkish Empire and divided into mandates by the League of Nations. As Britain received Transjordan and Palestine, so the French were given responsibility for what was known simply as Syria. But Moslem nationalists in Syria were pressing for independence and threatening to disrupt French commerce. As a result, in 1920 a new coastal state was created, based upon the pro-French Christian enclave around Mount Lebanon (from which it took its name) and designed to provide protection to the important trading routes of the eastern Mediterranean seaboard. In order to give the state geographical depth and at least a modicum of viability, a number of Moslem-dominated provinces of Syria had to be added, and this did in fact create a country in which the Christians only just retained a majority, but a carefully constructed constitution solved the problem. By tradition (enshrined in the National Pact of 1943), both the president of Lebanon and the commander-in-chief of the armed forces have always been Christian, while the prime minister is a Moslem. Such a compromise, in the nature of most such attempts, was not guaranteed to work indefinitely, particularly in the light of inevitable changes in the demographic balance of the state.

Lebanon officially gained independence in 1941, after British and Free French troops had overthrown the pro-Vichy colonial administration, although it was not until 1946 that the last of the French forces withdrew. They left behind an extremely vulnerable country, unnatural in its territorial boundaries and subject to irredentist claims from Syria as well as to all the pressures of communal division.

It was this lack of basic security, coupled to the continued Christian domination of the political leadership, that helped to create a rather luke-warm attitude towards the problems of the Arab world, characterised by a less than complete commitment to the conflict with Israel after 1948. Despite involvement in the 1948–49 campaign, Lebanon posed a

progressively diminishing threat to the security of Israel – in 1956, although announcing support for Egypt in the Suez crisis, she did not break off relations with Britain or France, two years later she requested and received military support from the United States, and her armed forces took no active part in the Arab-Israeli wars of 1967 or 1973. Indeed, as the Maronites tended to regard themselves and their country as more European than Islamic, the Israelis even found useful allies among the Phalangist militia of the Gemayel clan and the breakaway 'army' in the south of the country led by the cashiered 'Major' Saad Haddad. Of course not all Maronites were this extreme, but that did not prevent a popular perception

that the Christian community as a whole was 'anti-Arab' and 'anti-Palestinian'. By the same token, although it became accepted to associate all Moslems with the 'struggle for the liberation of Palestine from the Zionist enemy', many Arabs would have liked nothing better than to have seen the departure of the refugees and their armed protectors.

The PLO arrives

But Lebanon was never strong enough to resist the pressures of the outside world and when, in 1970, the PLO was forced by events in Jordan to find a new base within striking distance of Israel, the state was a natural choice, particularly as it had

Above: An M109A1 of the IDF on its way into the Lebanon in 1982. These self-propelled artillery pieces had a 155mm gun.

neither the will nor the means to resist the influx. The results were unfortunate, for the actions of the Palestinian guerrillas inevitably invited Israeli retaliation and forced Lebanon into the front line of confrontation between the Arabs and Jews.

This in turn led to clashes between armed guerrillas and the regular Lebanese Army (by now becoming dominated by Christians who, in the prevailing atmosphere of tension, forged links with the Phalangists) and undermined still further the delicate ethnic balance upon which the

constitution of Lebanon was based. The situation was not helped by overt interference by neighbouring Arab states, who forced Lebanon to grant the Palestinians full territorial rights over their own camps and unhampered transit or access southwards to the border with Israel. Thereafter, as Israeli retribution increased and intensified, Lebanese civilians and their property became the depressing casualties of a war which was not of their making.

After 1973 Lebanon was forced by Arab pressure to allow the PLO to protect their own camps and to deploy heavy weapons in their defence. This solved nothing and armed clashes continued as the Palestinians first influenced and then undermined the political structure of the Lebanese state. They helped radicalise the Moslem Left and formed 'alliances' with the disaffected Shi'ite and Sunn'ite groups within the country. When the Druze leader, Kamal Jumblatt, assumed the leadership of the leftist Moslem forces in Lebanon,

he moved even closer to elements of the PLO. Together they conspired to redress the constitutional balance of power and convert Lebanon into the main Arab confrontation state against Israel.

In the face of weak and increasingly ineffective central government, disenchanted Christian Maronites turned to the Phalange for support. Polarisation increased and a collision between the opposing factions appeared to be inevitable. When it came, each side blamed the other for provoking it. On Sunday, 13 April 1975, just after noon, a busload of Palestinians returning to the Tal az-Za'atar refugee camp to the east of Beirut was ambushed in the streets of the Ain ar-Rummanah suburb, a Phalangist stronghold. Twenty-seven men, women and children were killed, probably in retaliation for an earlier incident, also in Ain ar-Rummanah, when a jeep-load of Palestinians opened fire on a group of Phalangists, killing one and wounding several others. Communal violence spread

Above: A Palestinian woman begs a Phalangist militiaman for her life in 1976. Opposite: Phalangist irregulars.

quickly and the largely Christian-officered Lebanese Army was deployed onto the streets to restore order. Instead, Moslem junior officers rebelled and were soon joined by elements of the rank and file. The country drifted inexorably into chaos.

Yasser Arafat and the mainstream of PLO leadership, who had hitherto sought resolutely to remain above the battle, were now dragged into the war. The one thing that they had tried to prevent was upon them, namely a dissipation of their strength in a struggle against the wrong enemy in the wrong place and at the wrong time.

Syria changes sides

In this most complex of civil wars the Syrians were first invited to intervene by

able to capitalise on this and establish a hegemony over the predominantly Shi'ite population around and to the south of the Litani River. Worried about this surrogate Israeli presence, the PLO, Lebanese and Syrians appear to have made a tacit agreement to allow the PLO to reassert itself in the region. A secret agreement between Yasser Arafat and the Syrian government reopened the supply route to the south from Syria – the so-called 'Arafat trail'. Many of the PLO units began to return to aid the embattled leftist and Shi'ite forces that were fighting Haddad. By the end of March 1977 a full-scale war was taking place.

The situation worsened throughout April and May, leading to greater Israeli involvement over the Lebanese border in support of Haddad. On 21 September the Lebanese president, Elias Sarkis, openly accused Israel of deploying American-built M–48 and M–60 battle tanks inside his state, and this was enough to suggest the likelihood of escalation, particularly as the Syrians were pressing for permission to extend their 'peacekeeping' efforts, in the guise of the Arab Deterrent Force (ADF), to the area south of the Litani. On 26 September, concerned at the potential for international crisis of these events, the United States successfully mediated a ceasefire.

Unfortunately this did not last. During the rest of 1977 and the early months of 1978 there were renewed and continual clashes, leading to more intense outbreaks of fighting. Israeli forces continued to aid the Phalangists and even staged a few raids of their own by land and sea. Occasional rocket attacks by the Palestinians against Israeli villages brought retaliation by artillery bombardments from across the border or from IDF positions inside southern Lebanon.

While all this was going on, the internal problems of Lebanon intensified, with different groups on both the Christian and Moslem sides struggling to assert or retain positions of power. In the south, Shi'ite Moslems, particularly around the port of Sidon, began to turn against the Palestinians, while in Beirut the Christians displayed growing resentment at the continued presence of Syrian/ADF forces in the capital and elsewhere, despite the

the Lebanese government, in support of the Moslem and PLO alliance against the Christians. However, when this force appeared to be on the point of gaining too complete a victory in May 1976, the Syrians abruptly changed sides and supported the Christian Lebanese government. The last thing that Damascus wanted was a PLO mini-state beyond its reach and influence, pursuing policies which could only rebound on the Arab world.

The Syrian intervention was a long-drawn-out and painful affair which required the tacit support of the Israelis to succeed. Syria could not deploy the size of force which would have produced a quick victory, for fear that this would either alarm the Israelis or cause the government in Damascus to fall; heavy and much-publicised casualties among the Moslems and Palestinians were equally unacceptable. The eventual ceasefire on 16 October 1976 settled very little of consequence. By that time the damage

to life and property, especially in the cities, had been severe. Banks and commercial concerns abandoned Beirut and this once-splendid city ceased to be the financial centre of the Middle East. In the elegant hotels that survived the civil war, relief agencies occupied the rooms once used by tourists. The Syrians maintained a large presence (up to 20,000 troops, plus artillery and surface-to-air missiles) under the umbrella of an Arab League peacekeeping force, and the Lebanese government virtually ceased to function. Private armies proliferated on both sides of the religious and ideological divide and the country prepared for the next round of a seemingly endless civil war that no-one could win.

Major Haddad's forces

During the fighting, many Palestinian units had been drawn from the south towards Beirut. The Israeli-backed Phalangist force of Major Haddad had been

Opposite: Saad Haddad, the cashiered major who became the Israelis' ally in southern Lebanon, using Israeli arms to improve his own position. Above: The sort of support Haddad could rely on – long-range artillery bombards suspected Palestinian positions in the Lebanon.

fact that it was these troops that had prevented a leftist victory in the civil war. Fighting flared up throughout Lebanon and the Israelis began to express concern about the motives of the ADF. There was even a suggestion that the state should be partitioned, with the Phalangists taking the south and the Moslems the north, but this merely created a fresh wave of anti-Israeli feeling. Renewed conflict seemed inevitable, and was not long in coming.

To the Israelis the prospect of heavy fighting in Lebanon, which could spill over into Galilee, was particularly worrying, and once the partition plan (which would have created a useful pro-Israeli buffer south of the Litani) had been rejected, there were few options left. The most obvious was put into effect on the night of 14/15 March 1978, when Israeli forces mounted a major invasion of southern Lebanon. Between 20,000 and 25,000 troops, supported by tanks, artillery, aircraft and gun-boats, crossed the border, ostensibly in response to a PLO raid into northern Israel three days earlier. An IDF spokesman said on 15 March that the intention was to establish a 10km (6-mile) security zone, although the fact that Israeli aircraft struck well north of the Litani, bombing Palestinian refugee camps at Shatila, Sabra and Burj al-Barajneh, implied a wider, anti-PLO, aim. During these raids the Israelis used American-supplied 'cluster bombs' – lethal containers which showered hundreds of small bomblets indiscriminately over a wide area – even though there was an agreement that they would not be deployed against civilian targets.

UNIFIL and peacekeeping

The loss of international support which this disclosure produced probably persuaded the Israelis to accept a UN Security Council resolution of 19 March which called for an end to the fighting and the imposition of a special peacekeeping force to create a buffer between the IDF and the Lebanese. The first unit of UNIFIL (the United Nations Interim Force in Lebanon) arrived on 22 March and on 7 April the Israelis announced plans for a partial withdrawal of their forces. This was carried out on 11 and 14 April and UNIFIL troops took over the Israeli positions. After initial clashes with the UN troops, the PLO also agreed to accept the cease-fire.

After the Israeli withdrawal, there were frequent accusations levelled at the UNIFIL troops that they were allowing Palestinians to infiltrate through their lines into Israel. The contingent from Eire was even accused of aiding the PLO,

and this led to a series of attacks upon the Irish troops by members of Haddad's Phalangist army. The situation was not helped by the fact that the Israelis would not allow the UNIFIL force to enter the Christian enclaves in southern Lebanon, claiming that the UN was there 'to prevent terrorist infiltrators' not to 'oppose the defenders of the Christian areas'. The effect of this was the same as preventing the Syrian/ADF troops from operating south of the Litani: it created a political vacuum in southern Lebanon which Haddad was able to fill. A Phalangist-controlled buffer zone – exactly what the Israelis had been aiming for – thus developed between Israel and the UNIFIL contingents, stretching from Naqoura on the coast to the Syrian border southeast of Marjayoun.

A pattern emerged, which was to last until mid-1982, throughout the country. UNIFIL troops were attacked sporadically by Haddad's forces and accused continually by the Christians and Israelis

of aiding the PLO or of permitting them to pass through the UN positions. There is little evidence to support these claims, but the fact that they were made at all implied that the situation was far from secure. Lebanon as an independent state had, to all intents and purposes, ceased to exist and had been replaced by a series of 'mini-states' each under the control of a different faction.

The PLO and their allies occupied a belt north of the UN positions from the Syrian border to the coast, curving north in a narrow strip through Damour to southern and western Beirut. The Phalangists controlled an area from eastern Beirut up the coast to Batroun and extending inland to Mount Lebanon. The rest of the country was under the Syrian/ADF forces. In addition, within each faction, rival groups were fighting for influence, and the inter-communal violence which had characterised so much of Lebanon's recent history continued unabated. Phalangist-led Christians fought constant

The F-15 Eagle, supplied by the United States, was to be one of the great successes of the Israeli campaign of 1982; in conjunction with new radar techniques involving AWACS aircraft over the Mediterranean, F-15s outfought the Syrian aerial forces. Opposite top: An Israeli Eagle returns to base. The large airbrake panel (displayed here) makes drag shutes unnecessary. Opposite left: The underside of an F-15 revealing its armament of Sidewinder and Sparrow air-to-air missiles. Opposite right: An F-15 releases its bomb load. Its maximum load was an enormous 7258kg (16,000lb) of bombs. Above: An F-15 climbs with its afterburners at full blast.

battles with the Syrians, particularly in and around Beirut, while the PLO, with Moslem and Druze support, took every opportunity to carry the war into northern Israel or, if that was not possible, into the areas controlled by the Christians. In response, in 1979, Major Haddad declared the region under his control to be 'independent free Lebanon'.

The decision to invade

Despite this development, however, the Israelis were far from happy about the situation on their northern border. It would appear that they favoured a Phalangist-dominated Lebanon, but the continued presence of the PLO and ADF clearly made this an impossibility. In such circumstances, there was only one viable option left and that was to use military force to remove the Arabs – the PLO as well as the representatives of the more legitimate states – and impose the

sort of political settlement required. At first, the international community seemed determined to prevent any such escalation. In 1980, for example, an Israeli armoured column which advanced into Lebanon in response to a guerrilla attack on a Jewish settlement in northern Galilee was halted by the weight of world opinion as expressed through the United Nations. But as time went on and world attention shifted away from the Middle East towards new trouble-spots in Poland and the South Atlantic, the Israelis moved.

The excuse for action came on 4 June 1982 when Shlomo Argov, the Israeli ambassador to London, was shot and very seriously wounded as he left a diplomatic reception at the Dorchester Hotel. His assailants were captured and eventually put on trial – they proved to be Arab students travelling on Iraqi and Jordanian passports – but this was immaterial to the Israelis. Their response was immediate. Over the next two days Israeli aircraft struck at Palestinian targets in Beirut and helicopter gunships attacked refugee camps just across the border. At the end of this 'softening-up' process, on 6 June, IDF armoured formations swept the UNIFIL troops aside and pushed north in a two-pronged advance deep into Lebanon. Under the codename 'Operation Peace for Galilee', the original aim was stated to be the establishment of a 40km (25-mile) security zone, jointly administered by Israeli and Haddad forces, but as the advance continued it became apparent that there was more to it than that. The 'hawks' in the Israeli Cabinet, led by Defence Minister Ariel Sharon, were determined to solve the problem of

Lebanon once and for all by destroying the PLO and forcing the Syrian/ADF contingents to withdraw. As always in Israeli strategy, the campaign needed to be swift and ruthless, both to avoid excessive IDF casualties and to ensure that sufficient gains had been made by the time that the inevitable international ceasefire was imposed.

The advance was spearheaded by the Israeli Air Force (IAF), which quickly gained local air superiority by destroying Syrian SAM-6 missile sites in the Beqaa Valley and fighting off a challenge from MiG-25s. This allowed fighter/ground-attack aircraft, bombers and helicopters to provide close support to the ground columns, which pushed ahead against PLO resistance.

On the coast, Centurion battle tanks and mechanised infantry units took the port of Tyre and then linked up with other forces that had come ashore at Sidon in an amphibious landing. As they moved on to Damour and the outskirts of Beirut, the second armoured column thrust northwards through the mountains, bypassing PLO locations and leap-frogging ahead using heliborne infantry. On 7 June a pitched battle had to be fought by these troops to overcome the formidable PLO stronghold at Beaufort Castle, but once that had been taken, the road to the north was open. Meanwhile, other IDF units followed the main advance, mopping up remaining PLO pockets of resistance, particularly in the towns. It was a costly business which resulted in high IDF casualties and enormous damage to Lebanese property, especially in Tyre and Sidon.

Left and below: The Merkava tanks first saw action during the drive into the Lebanon in 1982. Opposite: The routes of the Israeli advance in 1982 and the siege of Beirut.

The Merkava in action

On 9 June the Israelis opened a third axis of advance as armoured units, equipped with the new and untested Merkava main battle tank, swung eastwards and outflanked the Syrian 1st Armoured Division in the Beqaa Valley. Infantry secured the high ground while the tanks moved into the valley itself to take on the Syrian T–62s and T–72s. Their way was eased by a superb series of IAF strikes which took out the last of the SAM–6s and managed to destroy a reported 29 of the Syrian MiGs that rose to oppose them. No Israeli aircraft were lost. The inevitable armoured battle took place around Lake Karoun on 11 June and the Syrian tanks proved no match for the Merkavas. The Syrian threat was effectively removed.

Meanwhile, the main Israeli advance on Beirut had reached the road junction at Khalde, south of the city, where the Palestinians, supported by Moslem militiamen, attempted to make a stand. But by now the momentum of the IDF was equal to the task and within hours the armour had pushed through to link up with Christian troops in the southern suburbs. The Phalangists guided the tanks through the streets of East Beirut as far as the 'Green Line' which divided the Christian (eastern) sector of the city from the Moslem (western) part. By first light on 11 June, with Israeli artillery and self-propelled guns deployed within range of the international airport, Beirut was encircled and an estimated 7000 Palestinians, together with remnants of the Syrian 85th Tank Brigade and sundry Moslem units, were trapped. Announcing complete success for 'Operation Peace for Galilee', the Israelis readily accepted a ceasefire. The price had been high – the Israelis admit to 100 dead and 600 wounded – but the threat posed by the PLO had been countered.

But the problem had not been solved entirely. PLO units, although surrounded, still existed and, in face of mounting international pressure and widespread condemnation of Israeli actions because of the civilian casualties involved, it was apparent that the only long-term solution would be the physical removal of the PLO from Lebanese territory. Thus, although the IDF maintained the military pressure on Beirut by mounting air and artillery strikes against the western sector, it was in Israeli interests to accept a more permanent settlement. This was reinforced by the fact that, as always, the country could not afford to keep her forces mobilised for long periods, and brought home with a vengeance when IDF casualties began to rise in skirmishes with the PLO in the labyrinths of high-rise apartments and narrow streets.

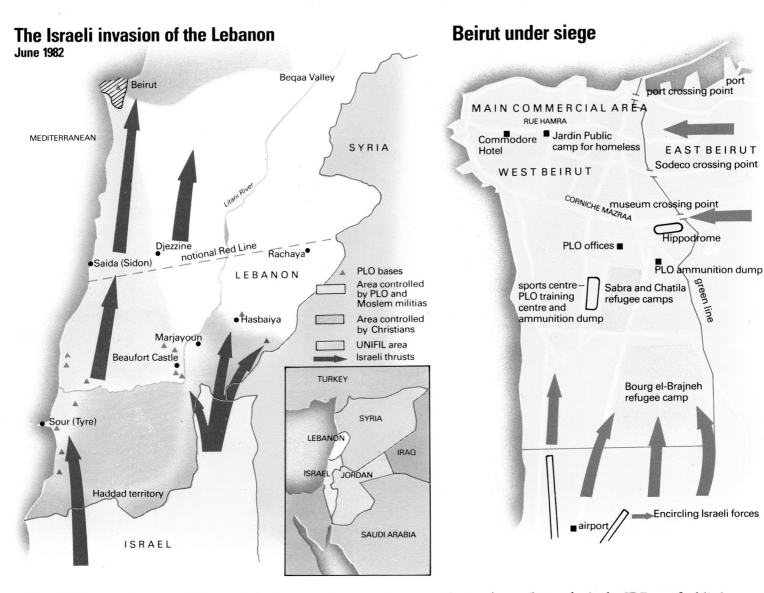

The Israeli invasion of the Lebanon
June 1982

Beirut

MEDITERRANEAN

Beqaa Valley

SYRIA

Litani River

Djezzine notional Red Line Rachaya

Saida (Sidon)

LEBANON

PLO bases

Area controlled by PLO and Moslem militias

Area controlled by Christians

UNIFIL area

Israeli thrusts

Hasbaiya

Marjayoun

Beaufort Castle

Sour (Tyre)

Haddad territory

ISRAEL

TURKEY

SYRIA

LEBANON

IRAQ

ISRAEL JORDAN

SAUDI ARABIA

Beirut under siege

port

port crossing point

MAIN COMMERCIAL AREA

RUE HAMRA

Commodore Hotel

Jardin Public camp for homeless

EAST BEIRUT

WEST BEIRUT

Sodeco crossing point

CORNICHE MAZRAA

museum crossing point

Hippodrome

PLO offices

PLO ammunition dump

green line

sports centre – PLO training centre and ammunition dump

Sabra and Chatila refugee camps

Bourg el-Brajneh refugee camp

airport

Encircling Israeli forces

In mid-August the terms of a settlement hammered out by President Reagan's special envoy Philip Habib were agreed by all concerned. PLO armed units were to leave Lebanon and go to other Arab countries away from Israel. Their withdrawal would be policed by a multi-national force of American Marines, Italian infantry and French troops, including the crack 2nd Parachute Regiment of the Foreign Legion, and they would also attempt to keep the peace until a reconstituted Lebanese Army could move into the areas vacated. The IDF would also withdraw to the south of Beirut and eventually leave Lebanon altogether.

In September 1982 the armed members of the PLO left Beirut, handing over many of their heavy weapons to Moslem groups which remained behind. There had been assurances from all sides that the non-combatant Palestinians would not suffer by having no-one to protect them.

Events took a nasty turn on 14 September when the president-elect of Lebanon, Bashir Gemayel, who had latterly become more accommodating towards his former Lebanese and Palestinian enemies, was assassinated. Who actually murdered him is still not known for sure – because of his position and policies it could have been anyone from the Syrians to disaffected Maronites – but the event was explosive and a Phalangist reprisal against the parties they would decide to blame was widely expected. In these circumstances, the laxity shown by the IDF towards the defence of Palestinian refugee camps at Sabra and Chatila is difficult to explain. The camps were in areas taken over by the IDF when they moved into West Beirut on 15 September and yet Phalangist militiamen (there is an unconfirmed consensus that they were Haddad's men) were allowed to enter them unmolested.

In the butchery that followed (16/17 September), the IDF can find little comfort, for the Israelis did nothing to prevent it or to stop it once it had started. The Israeli government was similarly indolent, provoking the bitter remark from one *Knesset* deputy – himself a former concentration camp victim – that it seemed to him like a 'final solution to the Palestinian problem'. Under considerable domestic pressure, Prime Minister Begin was forced reluctantly to convene a commission of inquiry, chaired by Judge Kahan. He found evidence of indirect complicity and culpability on the part of IDF officers and troops, as well as members of Begin's government. Sharon was forced to resign as Defence Minister (although he retained his Cabinet rank) and a number of military officers including the IDF chief of staff, Rafael Eitan, suffered an unwelcome glare of international publicity, although in the end Prime Minister Begin himself managed to survive.

Meanwhile, the problems of Lebanon persist, with the IDF and the multinational peacekeeping force providing two more actors in the tragedy. Lebanese groups are still fighting each other; the IDF is continuing to lose soldiers in ambushes mounted by Shi'ites and Druzes in the south of the country; the Phalangists, with Israeli support, are trying to suppress Moslem enclaves in the Chouf mountains; and the Syrian/ADF forces are still in position to the north of Beirut. The IDF refuses to vacate the country until unattainable demands are met and the Phalangists of Beirut, owing allegiance to the new president, Bashir Gemayel's brother Amin, are giving signs that they would favour an end to the Israeli alliance. They seem to have given up their demands for partition and be aiming towards greater integration into the Arab world – a discovery of identity which could have far-reaching consequences. All in all, it seems fair to say that the war in Lebanon is far from over, and the attack on the American Embassy in April 1983 bore witness to the Lebanon continuing as the focus of Middle East tension.

During the Israeli advance into Beirut, the city suffered heavily as it was bombarded (main photograph) and many of its inhabitants were killed or made homeless (inset opposite top). The main damage was done by heavy artillery (inset opposite centre). Inset opposite bottom: An Israeli radio operator. Inset right: Israeli mobile artillery moves through West Beirut. The Israeli advance was not unresisted: PLO anti-aircraft guns (inset bottom centre) maintained a barrage against the Israeli Air Force, while rockets (inset bottom right) were used to answer Israeli artillery.

The prospects for peace in the Middle East are therefore little brighter now than they were in 1948. An embattled Israel has still to find lasting security, the PLO has yet to attain even the beginnings of its political demands and the Arabs continue to squabble among themselves. The ingredients of conflict, mixed into the cocktail of war on so many occasions over the last 35 years, are present to a degree which makes future tragedy virtually inevitable.

Bibliography

A. J. Barker, *Arab-Israeli Wars*, London 1981 (1948–73)
P. Calvocoressi, *World Politics Since 1945*, London, 4th edn. 1982
T. Clarke, *By Blood and Fire*, London 1981 (King David Hotel, 1946)
D. Hirst, *The Gun and the Olive Branch*, London 1978 (1917–75)
C. Herzog, *The War of Atonement*, London 1975 (1973 War)
C. Herzog, *The Arab-Israeli War*, London 1982 (1948–73)
W. Laqueur, *Confrontation, The Middle East War and World Politics*, London 1974 (1973 War)
K. Love, *Suez, The Twice-Fought War*, London 1970 (1956 War)
E. Luttwak and D. Horowitz, *The Israeli Army*, London 1975
P. Mangold, *Superpower Intervention in the Middle East*, London 1977
E. O'Ballance, *The Sinai Campaign*, London 1959 (1956 War)
E. O'Ballance, *The Third Arab-Israeli War*, London 1972 (1967 War)
E. O'Ballance, *No Victor, No Vanquished*, London 1981 (1973 War)
Sadat, Anwar el-, *In Search of Identity*, London 1978
H. Thomas, *The Suez Affair*, London 1970 (1956)
Thompson, Sir Robert (ed), *War in Peace, An Analysis of Warfare since 1945*, London 1981

Index

Figures in italics refer to captions